How to Work in
BEVELED GLASS

How to Work in
BEVELED GLASS

Forming, Designing, and Fabricating

Anita and Seymour Isenberg

Chilton Book Company Radnor, Pennsylvania

Copyright © 1982 by Anita and Seymour Isenberg
All Rights Reserved
Published in Radnor, Pennsylvania 19089, by Chilton Book Company
and simultaneously in Canada by VNR Publishers,
1410 Birchmount Road, Scarborough, Ontario M1P 2E7

Manufactured in the United States of America
Designed by William E. Lickfield

Library of Congress Cataloging in Publication Data

Isenberg, Anita.
   How to work in beveled glass.

   (The Chilton glassworking series)
   Includes index.
   1. Glass craft.   I. Isenberg, Seymour.
II. Title.   III. Series.
TT298.I828   1982   748.2′028   81-69047
ISBN 0-8019-7103-9   AACR2
ISBN 0-8019-7104-7 (pbk.)

Front cover: Dome, 16′ diameter, made of 5,500 pieces of beveled and stained glass, by
Steve Williams. Back cover: *Exercise #59*, painted, fired and beveled glass on black glass,
by Carl Powell, copyright © 1981, 21″ × 25″.

All photographs of Barbara Basham's work in the color section taken by Brian Patarich,
Phlogiston Photographics, Boulder, Colorado.

1 2 3 4 5 6 7 8 9 0   1 0 9 8 7 6 5 4 3 2

To
Faye *and* Milt
who take our minds off it

"... did he win
the hearts of all that he did angle for."
Shakespeare, *Henry IV*, Part 1

Acknowledgments

A great number of people cooperated with us during the writing of this book. Many are named in the succeeding pages, among them the artists who contributed descriptions of their working methods and photographs of their work, and the manufacturers who gave generously of their knowledge and equipment. Above and beyond such gracious provisioning of our beveled glass larder are the efforts of still other individuals who volunteered their time, their advice, and—in one case—his home, to make our efforts more comfortable and precise. In all areas we were met with kindness and consideration, and an eagerness to get the book on the market and the information disseminated. In this regard we would especially like to thank Chris McCall of Denver Glass Machinery for allowing us free rein to poke and pry all through his factory, and for his patience with our many requests. We are indebted, as well, to Linda Neely of Prism Glass for demonstrating many procedures for our camera and for her minute perusal of the manuscript. She was also our authority for the questions and answers in the interludes. Many of these came from the *Beveling Glass Quarterly*, which she edited.

To Steve Williams of the Denver Stained Glass School we are doubly beholden. First for the grounding in the history of beveling, secondly for the airing over the mountains to Aspen, piloting us among the pitfalls of the first and the crags of the second with professionalism and eclat.

Contents

How to Work in
BEVELED GLASS

Introduction

In this book we will be discussing hand-beveled glass. We stress the use of the word *hand*, because hand-beveled glass does require the use of a machine. You can't just sit with a piece of Carborundum paper and rub and knock your angles into shape. There probably wouldn't be much left of you after two bevels—and what there was would quickly lead you to another craft or to some therapeutic device.

So some sort of machine is necessary. And machines require expense, although it is one that is fairly rapidly made back in the joy and profit of the craft. There are very few crafts that do not require an initial outlay of some sort. A beveling machine is probably one of the least expensive from the standpoint of productivity and steadfastness. Good beveling machines last forever.

We broach the subject because you may well ask—as we have been asked—if what we are doing is machine work, why do we call it "hand beveling"? We do so because in the techniques we describe the hand, not the machine, is primary. The hand, the eye, and the concept are the dominating factors. The machine only helps to carry out the concept. And the machine is always, without exception, guided by the hand. That means you, the craftsperson, remain in control of what you create. The machine is a convenience. You cannot depend on the machine to do your work. It has been designed only to do its own.

There are a number of beveling machines on the market, and we will attempt to cover as many as we can. Each of them requires particular techniques to get the best out of them. But their best is dependent on *your* best. In the long run, a machine that suits you actually becomes a part of your crafts personality. It helps you to create a statement—a *planned* statement—much in the way that a typewriter does. Yet no one would argue that the typewriter creates the pattern of the words. But the beveling machine does not create the design of the bevels, or their angles, or their style. The craftsperson does that.

So whatever machine you decide to purchase or rent, there is both investment and responsibility involved. Every machine has its own particular idiosyncracies. You should learn to make these work for you, and not let them work against you. The machine doesn't know any better, but you do. You must practice with your machine, experiment with it, find out its capabilities and limitations in relation to your own. It never creates—that's your job. Even the mammoth line-beveling machines that turn out miles of beveled glass just for the sake of the end result are still dependent on a designer's concept of the result.

That is not to imply because a machine is involved that the beveling process is particularly difficult. Reduced to its essentials, it is simplicity itself. What you are doing is using a set of grinding wheels to shape the glass edge and then polish it back to conform with the rest of the glass surface, developing a prism effect in the edge. However, within that simplicity, as in all crafts, lies the devil of oversimplification. In fact, good beveling takes coordination between the hand and the eye. It also takes patience in the quest for perfection and a pleasure in design. Add to that the fun of watching a plain, ordinary piece of plate glass become a thing of beauty.

Beveling, today, is going through a rejuvenation with the rest of the stained-glass field. Used in combination with stained glass, or used in colored beveled pieces, it provides a moving artistic experience. In its own terms, that of relating strictly to noncolored or clear glass, beveling provides a depth to the play of light on its surface as well as the dramatic impact of the explosion of light along its edges. But these are only a few of its uses. Given the flexibility of the material, the mutability of light, the imagination of the craftsperson and the pleasure the eye takes in being enlightened, the uses of beveled glass as an artform are practically endless.

It is therefore surprising that, until now, there has not been a textbook about the craft. Yet curiosity about beveling and beveled glass popularity has in recent years taken a decided upward turn. Such curiosity has been forced to feed on the overly technical and occasional articles appearing sporadically in professional journals. Certainly there has been nothing for the crafts or hobby person to be guided by.

We have endeavored to provide such a guide here as well as developing a working manual for the reader who may already be involved in the craft. Our approach is to assume the reader knows nothing at all about what we are teaching. In beveling, as in most other glass work, it's better to start from scratch.

That is not to say that this is strictly a "beginner's" book. It is a book for anyone who is interested in glass beveling. No doubt as soon as it is published—as generally happens with our books—other books on the same subject will appear. That's fine with us; the more the merrier. It would certainly be better than the void that presently exists.

We present what we believe to be a selection of very good beveled artistry in Part II. Even so, it is possible that the best work in beveled glass is yet to come—possibly from these very same artists. If so, it will still be based on the processes and techniques you will find described and illustrated here.

Prologue: The Search for a Lost Craft

The history of beveling is somewhat vague. The craft—for that is how it started—appears to be more or less a direct descendant of glass grinding. This was a craft that reached its apogee in cut crystal. Actually the notion of putting a tapered, polished edge on a piece of glass—which is what beveling is—did not develop from any artistic urge, but rather for a technical purpose. English manufacturers of scientific instruments as far back as the early 1800s used glass where they could because it was easy to keep clean. They found that grinding glass stoppers and bottle necks not only provided a tight fit, but allowed for hermetic air-sealing within the bottle. The stopper wouldn't fall out even when the jar was inverted. Ground-glass stoppers were used in pipetting devices as well, where small amounts of liquid were to flow. These turnable stoppers allowed for easy motion but prevented any extra drops from getting through except where the hole was drilled. The English and the French still argue today over which country discovered beveled glass. It is the least important of their arguments, but there is a certain comfort in knowing that it is important enough to remain a controversy.

A Decorative Art

Taking things a step or so further, beveling eventually became a decorative device. In fact, it was decorative long before it became "artistic." We turn again to the old-time English manufacturers of scientific instruments. A number of their instruments can be found in museums, crude electronic ancestors of things we take for granted today. Holes were ground in glass to hold the various components, which were neatly placed inside. Of course glass offered a small coefficient of expansion aside from being easily kept clean, and it allowed you to see what was going on inside as well. But in addition to that, these instruments were designed to be pleasing to the eye. Often the workers beveled the glass plate of the instrument—which was a fairly thick glass for sturdiness—and this made it easier to encase in a bezel so that it could be attached to something. This, in turn, made it more convenient to use. Here is an instance where function and design go hand in hand.

In the United States glass beveling became popular in the early 1900s, and most of the beveled glass was turned out in Chicago. Many other cities claim their importance in the business—New

Orleans, for instance—but judging by the mail-order catalogues still to be found in quantities, architectural beveled and stained glass was mainly made in Chicago.

An Industrial Art

If you were to visit an industrial glass factory, you would see production divided into strict compartments. The glass grinding, for instance, would be a department of its own. This one section in its two or three aisles might encompass more than 250 square feet, with grinding stations on either side of each aisle. These were all belt-driven machines of course, since this was way before the use of electric motors. But the machines were efficient nevertheless.

At each machine sat a man whose only function was to grind off the excess glass from each blank to give the bevel its initial shape—what we call today "roughing" the bevel. Every so often men would come down the aisles with large pushcart stands and pick up the rough pieces of glass and distribute new blanks. The roughed pieces would be taken to the next aisle of fifty or sixty operators, who would do the next step in the process—smoothing the glass. And from there the glass was taken to the polishers in still another aisle. One particular type worker did not know another man's job. This was not to keep the overall process secret, but rather for efficiency's sake. It would have been counterproductive to have one person do each and every step.

After the bevels had been cork-wheeled and polished, they went to still another area for assembly and crating. Overall production here furnished beveled glass windows in multitudes. Every day scores of them were shipped all over the country. These were not just bland, factory-made reproductions. Some were highly individual, many were lovely, and intricacy was the order of the day. They could also be expensive—as much as two or three dollars a linear foot.

Beveling, then, was regarded as a work process, hardly an art form so far as both the technique and the creation of the final result were concerned. Even the finest beveled windows were accorded the status of decoration, not fine art. The craftsmen were poorly paid and probably thought of their trade as inferior to that of the plasterer or mason. Certainly it did not have the aura of bricklaying. It was strictly an assembly-line process. Probably few, if any, workers bothered to look over the finished product. They worked to bring home a paycheck.

The major glass machinery manufacturer for beveling was the Henry Lang Company in Chicago. Before this company began to produce these units, a number of beveling plants had their own machines made specifically for them. But this could be time-consuming and quite expensive.

The Henry Lang Company was the only major manufacturer of glass machinery from 1890 to about 1930, when, with the advent of the Depression, glass beveling went into decline. Catalogues are still around that go back to 1890 for Henry Lang machines as well as for other companies. Within the next ten years, however, public interest in stained-glass windows came to the fore, since beveled glass was not considered to be anything special. Bevels were assembled into a cheaper form of art-glass windows than stained glass. Many factories also preferred to make stained-glass windows rather than beveled glass to avoid the expense of a beveling machine. The economics of producing the two types of windows were probably about the same as they are today—that is, the value of stained glass and beveled glass were equal to the value of the labor involved. But beveled windows hardly had the stained-glass "image."

The Henry Lang cast-iron machines were extremely large and heavy. Each beveling station was a separate entity, and each weighed about 650 pounds. Four stations were necessary in the beveling process. Initially these machines were belt driven, but as time went on many were converted to electricity. They were never driven by foot power because the grinding, smoothing, and polishing wheels were too massive to be worked by a treadle. The original power was delivered by way of a line shaft suspended from the ceiling of the factory. Every ten feet or so there would be a bearing assembly. A belt, either driven by a small steam engine or, in Chicago, by a municipal steam engine, was placed at the end of the shaft. This type of device could furnish a number of factories with power. If you were located in the industrial district and you paid your taxes, you would share an alleyway with other factories. Because there was some large source of steam power, you simply tapped into it.

Imagine those old days in one of these factories. Listen to those old leather belts, four or five inches wide—a joy to hear. Many of the old shops that had discontinued their beveling operation for lack of interest in the early 1870s began to use the machines again around the turn of the century. The line shaft was still operable, and now they could hook it up to an electric motor. Listen carefully and you can hear throughout the shop the leather belts ringing, the big flywheel turning, the slap, slap, slap of the leather belts, the turning of the wheels, the slap, slap, slap of those leather belts.

Contemporary Beveling

Man with a Quest

Steve Williams was not around when beveled glass went into a decline in the early 1930s. But about ten years or so ago beveled glass began to make a reappearance. It wasn't particularly dramatic, but some people like Steve Williams, who today runs the Stained Glass School in Denver, took notice and got curious. At that time Steve was dealing in architectural antiques, and among them were stained-glass and beveled windows. Occasionally he would see pieces of some of the old machinery and get the chance to talk to people who had been in the beveling trade. Soon he became so interested that he decided to learn the craft himself. But where could he go to learn? And learn on what?

At the time there was at least one plant in Milwaukee and several going back into business in Chicago, but it was a small dent in a generally bleak scene. Machinery was scarce, and most of the work being done was repair work, totally uncreative. Some of the very first people to begin doing original work were reluctant to let anyone know how they did it, or even what the general principles were. They would allow you to work for them as a grinder (read *apprentice* for some of the old stained-glass studios), but that was as far as you could get.

Then, coincidentally, a number of beveled windows began turning up in Colorado. Denver was the western city for architectural antiques between Los Angeles and Saint Louis, and just about the only such metropolitan center in that area in the early 1920s. A number of architectural antiques began to appear when people sold their homes and estates went up for auction. There were a number of architectural antique dealers in the city, at least two of them operating on a large scale. But they had a problem. Many of the beveled windows that they were buying from salvage companies were lovely, but they needed to be repaired. And no one around knew how to bevel glass, let alone how to repair it.

It was about that time that Steve, still wanting to learn how to bevel, heard about a shop in Colorado Springs that retained an old man who still knew what the beveling process was all about. In fact, he still had all the machinery. In 1970 Steve asked him if he would be willing to teach him.

The Fifteen-Minute Beveling Lesson

"This guy," says Steve, "had an old Henry Lang. And he was really a nice man, you know, no pretenses. He was willing to

Fig. 1 Steve smoothing a bevel on his large smoothing stone. As he works, he tips the bevel.

Fig. 2 Polishing the bevel on a vertical wheel.

teach. He told me he knew of an old Sommer and Maca combination machine, a 4-in-1, leather belt, converted to an electric motor. It was on a farm in Pueblo. A friend and I drove down, and the machine was actually there. You would never recognize it as such; it looked like a piece of old farm machinery. The farmer said the scrap value was $250. I had brought a trailer and borrowed some heavy iron rods to use as prods. I prodded the machine onto the trailer and took it home and plugged it in. It worked beautifully.''

We said, "You really wanted a machine."

"Badly."

Then Steve had his first beveling lesson. "The old guy taught me how to bevel in that he said this is the grinding station, this wheel grinds it a little better, this wheel puts some polish on it, and the next polishes it out finely. Go to it."

"That was your lesson?"

"That was it. The lesson lasted about fifteen minutes. So I produced some very crude bevels for about a year or so. I couldn't do inside curves because the grinding wheels were flat—horizontal. They are suitable for grinding only flat, long, straight lines and outside curves. On this machine the grinding and smoothing wheels were horizontal, and the two polishing stations were vertical. When you turned the thing on it all jumped to life at once. Everything whizzed, turned, and flew, lots of buzzers, bells, and widgets. I finally decided to find out how things were really done, so on an antique trip back East, I asked in an art glass studio if they knew anyone who could show me how to bevel."

"Oh, yes, they said. There's old Charley. He's still hanging on. Yes, he used to bevel. He'd be flattered and impressed if you express an interest. So I went off to find old Charley and, yes, he told me he beveled and how impossible it would be for me to learn, that it took thirty or forty years to get good at it. I mean you had to apprentice and get the hang of it. But he'd give me what he could in the way of information. Usually, after a little while these old-timers would open up and tell you everything they knew. You always had to use the same approach though. You had to be very humble and agree that there was no way you could ever learn to be as competent as they were, but you'd like to give it a try. After talking to half a dozen or so of these people, you'd find some who had a few of the old wheels, and they would either give or sell them to you. That was the key, you see. Once I had all the different little wheels necessary for making inside curves, I could do anything. The process is simple and rational, quite easy for anyone to do with the machine. But the machine is a very specific machine. You can't jury rig it or substitute for it. I tried using a lapidary machine, but it just wasn't suitable for glass. Glass is softer than rock and requires a different set of grinding wheels. Most important of all is the smoothing wheel. That is the key to the whole process."

The First Beveling School

Now that Steve had his machine and gradually began to master the beveling process, he found more and more people who wanted to know about glass—stained and beveled. He could teach stained glass readily enough since it didn't require a machine—but what about beveled glass? At this point he met a fellow enthusiast, Chris McCall, and they became partners.

"About nine months after we'd opened the stained-glass school, we decided to teach beveling," Steve recalls. "At this time there was some automatic beveling going on at Cherry Creek. They were just starting, using a Newcastle stone the size of a 150-gallon oil drum. It was a very slow process, and it would do the grinding and smoothing all in one operation. Our idea was to offer limited classes for beveling. Five days with a guarantee that you had to bevel perfectly when you were finished, or you could take the course again until you beveled perfectly. Almost no one had to take the course again."

But the school had a problem. People were coming to learn on the machine, but what were they to work on when they got home? The school didn't sell machines. Students photographed the machine in the shop and then went home either to try and put one together on their own or have a machine shop re-create one for them. Hardly a satisfactory endeavor. Some people managed to find a machine here or there—mostly, again, in farmers' fields.

"One of our best students, Mark Bogenrief, found an old set of Henry Lang machines in a farmer's field and got there just in time before the farmer cut them up for scrap iron. But this was the exception. We were being deluged with requests for machines."

Steve finally took six months off and designed a machine, which he started producing in 1978. However, it was too massive for students and the average hobbyist. From this one, Chris McCall designed the present studio-model machine.

Beveling Machines for One and All

Chris McCall was a stained-glass enthusiast. He did not know enough about beveling to worry about what you could or couldn't do. That left very few restraints on his imagination. "I knew they did inside curves on round wheels, so I figured why not do straight lines on round wheels as well—that is, on vertical wheels. I asked Steve, and he said that it couldn't be done. You could do the roughing and the smoothing, but you couldn't go any further than that. Why? Well, I had to reduce the size of the machine, which meant reducing the size of the wheels, which meant upping the speed or you'd never get the work done. I fiddled with this and came up with a fair but by no means satisfactory bevel and a far from perfect wheel. Then Steve came up with a fiber wheel. Part of the reason we were having trouble was that the cork wheel kept throwing the pumice. It was so small that I had to get the surface speed up to a point where it just wouldn't hold the pumice. Other machines, Lang, for instance, had vertical cork wheels, but they were big, big wheels with lots of surface. They were 30" in diameter. I was trying to reduce this to a small studio 10" wheel. Big wheels can run slowly, but small ones can't. It was the fiber wheel that led to the successful machine we now produce. And of course we are not the only people making beveling machines now. But I believe we were the first. The first to teach beveling and the first to make machines for students and hobbyists. That's something to be proud of."

Questions by Way of Preface

The four of us had been having breakfast. We were up to coffee. A few questions still called for answers as prefatory remarks. Such as, Why bevel? What is the nature of beveling?

Steve: The purpose of beveling is to provide an interesting and rich texture and relief. This highly enhances any design. Secondarily, beveling provides a refraction of light that you can see not only on the piece of art glass itself, but you also get a very pleasing color wash on the floor. Refraction breaks light up into its constituent colors, which is at once very subtle and very dramatic.

Q: Well, if that's the case, why not use a highly leaded glass? Surely that would make the glittering and prism effect that much greater.

Steve: That would be very expensive—certainly too expensive for the average hobbyist. Perhaps in a technically highly polished piece of glass the difference would be obvious—a telescope, maybe. But in hand beveling it wouldn't stand out. In the long run you wouldn't be getting all that much effect for your extra money.

Chris: You certainly wouldn't. When you see a finely done window, where the bevels are all of high quality and they glitter and gleam because of the fine polishing, people say that it looks good because it was made of leaded crystal. Mark Bogenrief was displaying at the show in Chicago last year. He pays meticulous attention to the quality of the bevels in his windows. He likes to use $\frac{3}{8}$"-thick plate or $\frac{5}{16}$" plate, so his bevels do have this lovely quality. Mark was sitting like a salesman on his Oriental rug in front of his windows, and a man and woman came by. The man said to the woman that the windows looked so nice because they were leaded glass. "Those are old leaded-glass windows," he said. And Mark said, "No they're not, they're plate." So the man said, "Don't tell me, I know beveling and I know glass and I know those are leaded crystal windows." Mark said, "Look, I made the windows and I bought the glass from Pittsburgh Plate." But it didn't matter, the guy kept arguing and when they walked away, he still was not convinced.

Q: Well, forget leaded glass in windows then. But we're going to be talking about and demonstrating how to make glass jewels. How about using leaded glass for those?

Steve: Jewels can be highly leaded in some cases. This makes them heavier than regular glass of the same dimensions. But of course jewels have so many facets in addition to the innate sparkle that they will glitter more than a window with a single facet whether they are plate or leaded. Sure, you can use leaded glass for jewels. Leaded glass is softer and easier to work with than regular soda-lime glass. It polishes faster. But for sparkle, the added facets are what's important.

Q: The phrase "traditional beveling" keeps coming up lately. What does the phrase mean to you?

Chris: Traditional beveling versus . . . what? Well, honeycombing and all the surface textures were done seventy or eighty years ago. Imagination is the only factor that limits the kinds of surface you put on a piece of glass. I suppose when beveling was first done in the early 1800s, it was standard on a piece of glass to have some sort of angle around the edges, ground, and then polished back to a high state of polish. That seems to be what beveling was all about. But it can be other things, too. You can grind the glass anywhere and polish it or even not polish it.

Steve: You can bevel one side in the traditional way, or you can bevel both sides. You can bevel unevenly and not polish all of it, or you can polish only some of it. Of course someone used to traditional beveling can look at this and say, "This guy doesn't know what he's doing, he doesn't know how to bevel." I don't believe that. It all depends if the end result is beautiful or a mess.

Q: What about beveling and glue chipping? These two techniques seem to go hand in hand.

Steve: It depends on the effect you want to create. I don't think there's all that much you can do in combination. Maybe 10 to 15 percent of beveled glass is glue chipped. It's just another surface modification.

Q: What do you see coming up in the future? There's some talk about using more colored glass in beveled windows, and even for the bevels themselves.

Steve: I'd love one of the glass companies to do some float-colored plate. Some nice pastel shades. I think that is coming, if not from the big companies, from some of the small operations. You have to watch out for bad table marks that you then have to polish out. Think what could be done with fifteen pastel colors to work in. Much more exciting than clear glass. You can find some pastel glass around. Antique polished plate, for instance. And ship's mirrors. Often rose tints were used in ship's mirrors to give you a healthy look even when the ship was pitching up and down. Some Art Deco work was done with blue-tinted mirror, but that was mostly all manufactured after World War I. Nobody makes it now. It's nice when you find these colors, though, because you can get some nice effects. Of course this is all mirror.

So far as plain plate, many people don't know that there is a difference in the color between new and old plate glass. How old is old? Anywhere from 1900 to 1930. The factories had not yet perfected the technique of removing all the iron from the glass. The iron gives a green or yellowish tint to the plate, especially on the edge. Chemicals are put into modern plate to neutralize this. When you see new glass on edge, it looks dark blue. When you look through it, it seems respectably clear. The old plate glass looks clear until you see it next to a new piece. When you bevel that old glass, the green tint becomes rich and warm, whereas in the new plate glass, the bluish tint is cold. This is especially important when you use a piece of new plate glass to repair an old plate-glass window. Here the new piece really stands out. So all repair work on old windows involves going to the salvage yard to get some old plate glass. Preferably without scratches.

Q: Ah, speaking of scratches . . .

Chris: Yes, it's hard to find old plate glass that doesn't have scratches. The way Steve bevels, it doesn't matter. His glass only has to be clean on one side, since he bevels everything to a point— pencil bevels—so one surface is entirely new.

Steve: It's fun and interesting to use varying widths of bevels within the same piece of work. But here you have to be careful about the machine you use. Some machines on the market have a fixed angle for their beveling procedure, and a fixed angle limits you creatively. You are stuck with traditional bevels. You can't, for instance, do a pencil bevel, where the bevel itself varies in width because the angle needs to change. These things can be done readily only when the glass is free in your hand.

Chris: That's very important. Many people who have never seen beveling are amazed when they see true hand beveling. They think it must be hard to hold the glass at the proper angle against the wheel. In fact, it is easy to do. It's only a myth that some sort of jig or set angle or rest makes it easy to work well. I want to emphasize that that's just not the case. The most common question I'm asked when people see me beveling at a show is, "Oh, the glass isn't held by a jig? How do you do it so accurately?" But the hand and the eye are incredibly accurate. You need the freedom to make individual representations rather than machine-made representations.

Steve: Well, that's what a craft is. I don't mean to say that you can't change the angle at all on a fixed-angle machine, but that only varies your width of bevel depending on the thickness of the glass. You can't make a transition where the piece swerves around and comes to a point, for example.

Q: What would be the best piece of advice you would give to someone who knows nothing about beveling at all but would like to get into it?

Chris: That's easy. Get into it.

Steve: Sure. Begin.

PART I: Techniques

◆━◆

CHAPTER 1

Equipment and Materials

In order to bevel you will need several specific items. First is the beveling machine. You can choose among several that are on the market. The interest in beveling has grown so much that a number of manufacturers have begun turning out machines for students and hobbyists as well as, or in place of, the larger, more massive commercial models.

Reduced to basics, beveling is a process whereby the edges of a piece of glass are angled from some point on the surface to the rim. The process accentuates refraction of light. Light waves, which travel in straight lines, strike the surface of the glass and are reflected in a scattered pattern, which to the eye shows glistening and sparkle. Those coming through the glass bend, breaking up into their constituent colors. Thus a prism effect is produced, an actual coloration of the glass edges, which can throw a wash of color onto the floor or walls of the room depending on where the glass is placed. The effect, to say the least, is striking and, at most, overwhelming. While beveling in the past has been looked on as a decorative rather than a fine art, craftsmen working with the techniques today, combining their imagination with the principles, have come up with results that are little less than astounding. As usual, the glass does most of the work in providing dramatic effects, but even the novice can find practical works of art coming to life under his or her hand. From this aspect alone, the craft is immediately rewarding. As technique is refined with further use and experimentation, beveling becomes another essential modality in the armament of the craftsperson who works in glass as a total artistic expression.

What Is Beveling?

Beveling machines all operate in much the same way. The differences between them lie mainly in the areas of cost and convenience. The machines are meant to do two things to the glass:

Beveling Machines

13

Fig. 1-1 An automatic line-beveling machine. (Courtesy Cherry Creek Beveling and Jewel Co., Denver, Colorado.)

to shape the bevel (that is, to grind away excess glass until the proper angle is achieved) and to repair the damage that has been done to the surface of the glass by having had that angle ground into it. Both activities of the machines are propounded by the nature of glass itself. When glass is ground, it becomes opaque, sandy, and it will not transmit or reflect light to any practical degree. Therefore, the surface that has been ground must be rejuvenated to its former clarity. The first process is called "roughing," the second, "smoothing," the third, "semi-polishing," and the fourth, "fine polishing." We like to retain the distinction between polishing stages, although they are often combined as "polishing." Beveling machines are specifically meant to give you, in the most efficient manner possible, both steps of the process. Roughing is done at a single step or "station," but polishing is done sometimes in two, but usually in three, steps.

It is possible to buy a machine that is actually three machines or four machines in one, each unit being a separate entity. Or you can acquire a roughing station or a polishing station alone. These single-purpose units may serve well in commercial enterprises where a great deal of work is being mass produced, but they are barely acceptable in hobbyist studios. Here, some type of machine that combines all the necessary units would serve the purpose best. Our own choice, admittedly arbitrary, is the Denver Glass Machinery's Studio Model Beveler, which we use throughout the book, together with Denver Glass's IB–16. Both of these machines demonstrate almost all that can be done with the beveling process, not only so far as beginners and hobbyists are concerned, but also for studios interested in going into beveling as a production enterprise.

Cost of course is always a restrictive element. Here, too, our choice of machines are those that give reasonable satisfaction for the money. In addition, the cost is not out of the range of the average hobbyist. At the same time, it is essential to point out that there are other machines on the market, some of which are mentioned in the Appendix.

Since the beveling process is not a complicated one, it is more than possible for you to build your own machine. A lot depends on how skillful you are, however. One warning: Don't start the job if you don't feel qualified. For one thing, you can, as one individual we know of did, discover so many unanticipated complications that building the machine, rather than using it, becomes the hobby. If you think you still want to try, before you start inquire carefully about the cost of the necessary individual components—especially the wheels. You may decide it is cheaper in the long run to *buy* a machine.

Of course you may feel that before going to the expense of buying a beveling machine, or going to the expense and trouble of putting one together yourself, you would prefer to rent one. Some glass studios—although not many at this time—do have a rental service. One is the Bolton Studio in Houston, Texas. Undoubtedly other studios, as beveling becomes more and more of a hobby, will follow David Bolton's lead in this respect.

Finally, you can always buy a used machine. Although there is not exactly a surplus on the market, every so often a few appear in classified ads in hobbyist or glass journals.

Before you invest in a used beveler, you should ask a few questions aside from whether or not it is the right style for you. However, some things are obvious enough even to an inexperi-

Fig. 1-2 The interior of a sophisticated manufacturing plant that produces bevels and engraved glass pieces, glue-chipped glass, medallions, and other glass items. (Courtesy Cherry Creek Beveling and Jewel Company, Denver, Colorado.)

enced eye. Does the motor (or motors) work properly? Are the belts in good shape? Are the water hoses properly placed? The hoses should be clear of any electrical connections. Most important, what are the wheels like, and how many come with the machine? The wheels are the most expensive single elements of any beveling machine. At the same time, buying a used beveling machine is like buying a used kiln. There isn't all that much that can go wrong, and you could end up with a real find for comparatively little money. However, the demand for these items is increasing, so if you are going to look, start looking now.

Electricity

Electricity of course is not a piece of equipment, and it may seem odd to mention it here, but it is an important element in the beveling process. Most of us take electricity for granted. In beveling, you will be working with electricity and water. Manufacturers take this into consideration, and factory-made machines come properly grounded. It is a factor that *you* must remember to include in any "home-made" unit you either purchase or put together yourself. Water is far too good a conductor of electricity to allow for any possibility of an accident.

Not as potentially lethal a problem by any means, but still an annoying one if it arises, is purchasing a machine for studio use and finding that it doesn't work off a 110-volt house current as you assumed. Instead, it takes a 220 line. You can have an electrician bring a 220 line in for you, or you can use a 110 power converter, which converts a three-phase to a single-phase line, but it is still one more thing to do, as well as an additional expense that you may not have expected. This could start you off on your new hobby in a somewhat bitter frame of mind. If you begin this way, it is our experience that things in general start to go sour— and you may end your new career before you even begin. Since it is usually the little things that get to all of us, and since it is simple enough to check on this beforehand, check this in the beginning.

Plate Glass

One of the joys of beveling is working with material that would otherwise be useless, transforming simple, common glass into an object of beauty. Plate glass is easy enough to find. To start, you can pick up scraps from your local glazer. Or you may have odds and ends of glass already lying about your studio. You can pick up old and new plate glass from salvage yards. The same holds true for mirror, which is fun to bevel and gives fascinating effects. And of course, if worse comes to worst, you can always buy your glass. The point is that you don't absolutely have to. You usually will be using small pieces of glass, and such odds and ends should be easy to find no matter where you live. You certainly shouldn't be reduced to start your beveling experience by cutting up the top of the living-room coffee table for a supply of plate.

Plate glass comes in various thicknesses—from $\frac{3}{16}''$ (most stock bevels) up. It is nice to know that there is a wide range of choices when it comes to thickness. The design and style of bevel depends as much on the thickness of the plate as on the pattern of the cut. Most automatic machines (such as the massive line bevelers) use $\frac{3}{16}''$ plate and make what is called a "skin" bevel. This has a fairly thick edge, since only a minimum of glass is removed from the surface. There isn't that much of a prism effect here. The degree of slant of the angle determines the quality of the prism. To get a good prism effect, the glass would have to be additionally ground by the machine. However, the process would mean additional wear on the heads—and in some cases the manufacturers, who seek to do the bevels as cheaply as possible, aren't willing to do this. This is one reason why machine-made bevels can be rather disappointing.

You don't have to be afraid of wearing out the wheels on your beveling machine. Use thick plate glass to get a dramatic effect. A steeper angle (thicker glass) gives the best prism. The glass used in many old windows is $\frac{5}{16}''$ plate. The thickness range of many workers today runs from $\frac{1}{4}''$ to $\frac{3}{8}''$, and a number of artists like to work even in $\frac{3}{4}''$ or $1''$ glass, which includes colored dalles glass. Old plate glass, in particular, gives a warm sheen to the bevels because of the excess iron content in the glass. You may want to use this in conjunction with new plate, which provides a colder, bluish sheen.

You may also want to experiment by mixing different thicknesses of plate glass within a single project, using the variances for emphatic touches. Almost any combination of glass and thickness can be conjoined. The beveling can provide a common touch or set one group of elements apart from others. It is up to you. Once you acquire the technique, you will discover that it will quickly become part of your artistic "grammar."

Stained Glass

Stained glass can also be beveled. Usually flashed glass is used, since here the dramatic result of the second color (or clear glass) on the edges is probably what you are after. Most stained glass is about $\frac{1}{8}''$ in thickness, so it isn't possible to get a very steep bevel.

In beveling stained glass, the same procedures are used as in beveling plate. You may want to bevel colored glass that is not flashed, just to achieve a subtle shading of the basic color as a decorative frill. There is nothing wrong with doing this, although most of the work that we have seen has been disappointing. The distinction between the beveled and unbeveled surfaces is mostly shown by light passing through the glass, and even here we do not find the result to be worth all the effort. Of course, you may like it, but it works best in glass thicker than $\frac{1}{8}''$—in dalles, for instance.

Masks and Safety Glasses

More people talk about masks and safety glasses than actually use them. It is true that they can get in the way of normal physical performance—such as breathing and being able to see. Since you will be working with wet surfaces while beveling, you may find that a mask isn't all that necessary. However, a mask is absolutely essential when dressing a wheel, especially a felt one, and this item should be kept in the work area.

While plenty of glass dust is produced in the beveling procedure, very few particles get into the air because the dust has been combined with water from the machine. However, no one can give you a guarantee as to how much does get in the air and, consequently, into your lungs. Therefore, during routine beveling, a mask is strictly an individual preference. When working "dry," however, it would be foolish not to wear a mask. Both cork dust and felt dust are extremely irritating and dangerous, and both are in the air in heavy proportions when either of these wheels is being dressed (or "turned").

Safety glasses are something else again. Beveling is basically a messy operation. Especially when using the cork wheel and pumice, the pumice tends to fly about, spattering hair, skin, and eyes. In this case, safety glasses come in handy. Of course you will have to keep wiping them off, which can be a nuisance. Again, individual preference will have to carry the day. To avoid at least some of the dust stand alongside rather than directly in front of the wheel.

Aprons, Towels, and Rinse Buckets

Because beveling is a messy affair, it is not something to be done in your best suit or frock. The polishing aspect is especially a challenge so far as trying to keep the material on the wheel rather than on you. Cerium oxide and pumice are bad enough, but jeweler's rouge is particularly nasty, and many craftsmen don't like to use it at all because of the cleanup time it requires. Therefore, it is best to wear some sort of work apron even over your work clothes. This way, when you leave the studio, all you have

Fig. 1-3 A cutting and shaping unit for zinc came and other metals. This is strictly an item of convenience for large projects. Harry Bullock's Studio Model Beveler, shown here, was modified for zinc came cutting and notching.

Fig. 1-4 A special zinc-came cutting wheel can be attached to either end of the Denver Machinery Studio Model Beveler. The iron bar that forms a rest for the came is notched to allow for pressure against the wheel. This wheel has no guards, so great care must be exercised. Unless you are doing a large project, it might be best to cut the came by hand with a hacksaw.

to remove is the apron, and you won't be carrying debris from the wheels to other parts of the house.

Towels, of course, are very useful, and paper towels are absolutely essential. You can wrap your hair in a bath towel if you don't have a cap handy. And paper towels are indispensable for wiping off your bevel so that you can look for facets, a process that you will be repeating over and over. They are also good for cleaning your hands and glasses, whether safety or regular.

A dip bucket, or rinse bucket, is a useful item to have, and you should have a different one for each wheel. Separate buckets will help to avoid contamination from one wheel to the next by carrying up dirty water on the glass. Contaminating your wheels can be a disaster so far as good beveling is concerned. It is also a good idea to have the various wash buckets alongside you, rather than on the floor. Then you won't have to keep bending over whenever you rinse. The more comfortable you are, the more time you can spend beveling, not stretching cramped muscles.

Every time that you change wheels, make sure that you wash the glass well. It doesn't matter so much if you transfer from a finer grit to a coarser one—that is, go from cerium oxide to, say, pumice. But it does make a great deal of difference if you transfer coarse grit to a stone that uses a finer one, as in going from the roughing to the smoothing station.

You should have several cutters on hand that are specific for plate glass. Most glass-cutter manufacturers make cutters with wheels specially suited to plate, and it is important that you use one of these rather than one that was made for some other glass. While you will probably be able to use another type, you will be making

Cutters and Pliers

Fig. 1-5 A specially formed wheel for channeling zinc came. A flat iron surface provides a sturdy rest that supports the came as it is worked on.

your job more difficult in the long run. It is just as easy to start doing things right in the beginning as it is to do them wrong.

For beveling, you will need two kinds of pliers: a plate-glass-breaking pliers and a running pliers. Both of these items are standard in the armamentarium of the stained-glass craftsman, and you can continue to use what you have for plate glass as well. However, if you want to use fairly thick plate for more than merely occasional diversions, you should acquire a running pliers that is more substantial than those used for $\frac{1}{8}''$ stained glass. This will relieve some of the pressure on your hands, and you want to

Fig. 1-6 Notching the channel into the end of a piece of zinc came with a specially shaped Carborundum wheel. The Studio Model beveling machine furnishes the power.

keep your major effort toward beveling, not glass scoring and breaking.

Pittsburgh Plate Glass makes fine heavy-duty running pliers that are exceptional in their ease of running long score lines on heavy plate. You might find it more than worth your while to invest in a pair. As shown in Figs. 1-7 and 1-8, we tape the jaws of our PPP (Pittsburgh Plate Pliers) to avoid the possibility of the jaws scratching the glass.

As for breaking out the score, the pliers you already may be using for stained glass will be sufficient. You may have to work harder at the procedure depending on the thickness of the plate you use. We use our Diamond glass breaker and running pliers for anything up to $\frac{1}{4}$". Above that we use our PPP to run the score.

Anyone who repairs beveled glass windows has to be struck by the fact that most, if not all, are done with zinc came rather than lead. This doesn't mean that lead came was never used on beveled windows; it does mean that usually little, if anything, is left of them to repair. Lead came is too malleable to sustain the weight of the heavy plate. Pieces of this glass tend to fall out as the window begins to sag.

Zinc came is an important material if you intend to make full-length objects, such as beveled windows or mirrors, with your new beveling machine. Zinc came weighs one-third less than lead came. True, zinc is not as malleable, but it is not true—as many beginners or those who have never worked with zinc came believe—that in order to get the zinc around the glass you must heat it. In fact, you can make zinc came conform to most shapes of beveled glass with hand pressure alone; even small pieces of glass can be treated in this way. Only when you are working with circles or ovals could you have some trouble. In these cases, you may have to make the zinc malleable by heating it. Or, you may decide to use lead came in these areas only, fitting them into the overall design. Zinc came, of course, is extremely solderable.

Zinc Came Versus Lead Came

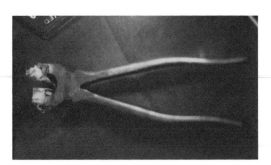

Fig. 1-7 The Pittsburgh Plate Glass running pliers. The jaws have been taped to avoid scratching the glass.

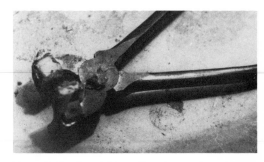

Fig. 1-8 Pittsburgh Plate Glass heavy-duty running pliers. Note the powerful jaws.

If you do have to heat the zinc came—if you are putting it around a small object such as a glass jewel, for example—a propane torch will work well. Don't touch the glass directly with the flame or you will crack it. Also make sure that you have a charcoal block or a firebrick under the zinc as you apply the torch. Otherwise, it is possible to set fire to the work surface when employing this technique.

Even using zinc came, you should still bar a large window, just as you would if you were using lead. Barring is done with galvanized metal formed to shape so that it interferes as little as possible with the design of the piece.

Chipping Glue

Many craftsmen like the combination of glue-chipped glass and beveled glass. The chipping and beveling technique is a Victorian idiosyncracy that is seeing a resurgence today; in fact, glue chipping alone has become very popular. The glue chipping breaks up the plain glass surface and sets off the beveling that much more. However, it's a technique that shouldn't be overused. The glue-chipping process itself is time-consuming, but it isn't complicated (see our book, *Crafting in Glass*).

One question that usually arises with the glue-chipping technique is, Do you glue-chip the glass first, or do you bevel first? It is generally agreed that it is better to glue-chip first and then bevel, since the glue chipping is the less precisely planned effect of the two, and it may not come out in quite the way you have in mind. One or both sides of the glass can be glue chipped, depending on the effect you are hoping to achieve. Any pastel-colored glass can be used, but the effect can be striking with clear glass as well.

Pumice, Silicon Carbide, and Cerium Oxide

Pumice, silicon carbide, and cerium oxide are abrasives that are applied to the glass surface with the various beveling wheels. Of the beveling wheels we will discuss, only two are used without any added abrasive: the smoothing wheel and the fiber wheel. There are specific reasons for this, and we will explain them in Chapters 5 and 7.

Silicon carbide is the coarsest abrasive. Anywhere from 80 to 120 grit can be put onto the cast-iron roughing wheel—the starting wheel. Grit becomes finer as the number goes up; 80 is a coarser grit, for instance, than 100; 100 is coarser than 120. You have to reach a compromise with yourself as to how coarse a grit you start with. The coarser the grit, the more rapidly it will abrade the glass, leaving a rough surface. If you begin with a grit that is too coarse, you will spend all the time you save on the roughing wheel, and possibly more, on the smoothing stone getting rid of this surface.

Pumice is a finer abrasive than silicon carbide, not necessarily in particle size but in hardness. Actually a type of volcanic glass, it is used for fine abrading. Dentists use fine pumice to clean teeth. Pumice comes in grades from extra fine to extra coarse. We suggest the use of a medium to coarse grit to aid in removal of facets from your glass that were not properly removed on the smoothing stone. The cork wheel, the third to be used, has a grit number of about 600.

The second wheel, or smoothing stone, uses no applied abrasive; the only abrasive is the wheel itself. The grit number of the smoothing wheel is 300 to 360, much finer than the 80 to 120 of the silicon carbide used on the roughing wheel. The last wheel, the felt polishing wheel, uses the abrasive cerium oxide, a fine powder. We use it at a grit of 1,000, which is very fine indeed. Many old-time bevelers used jeweler's rouge on the felt wheel. This is an iron oxide powder that works well as a polishing agent, but it is messy and few people use it anymore. It stains everything it touches, and stains on the skin have to wear off—you can't wash them off.

So, as you can see, the grit used in beveling gets finer and finer as each process leads to the next, and glass removal gets slower and slower with each process.

You might well ask the question, Why use all these different materials? Why not use silicon carbide for the entire process, merely substituting finer and finer grits? Well, you can do this. The old-time bevelers had three cast-iron wheels and a single felt wheel. They ran the glass down exactly in this manner, using finer grits of silicon carbide on each cast-iron wheel. This is actually faster, and in the long run it produces a more accurate bevel than with the method we have just described. Unfortunately, the weight of the old machines makes them difficult to move around, and the cast-iron wheels are awkward and require heavy supports and bases. Practicality of cost and space lies in favor of the first method, especially for hobbyists, but even for most commercial enterprises as well.

CHAPTER 2

Scoring and Breaking Plate Glass to Pattern

Many workers in glass, and good ones at that, shy away from working with plate glass that is more than $\frac{1}{4}''$ in thickness. Why? Because they are afraid of it—afraid it won't break properly, afraid they may get cut, afraid it will make them look foolish and non-professional. And there is some truth in each of these reasons. Measuring up to a thick piece of glass armed with only a standard cutter can be daunting.

Yet plate glass, even very thick plate glass, is not that difficult to deal with. So relax. As a prospective beveler, you will have to become acquainted with all of the idiosyncracies of glass, and you will find them easier to overcome than you think.

Selecting Your Glass

Before choosing a piece of plate glass for beveling, consider the following:

1. Is it the proper thickness for what you want to do? Don't worry if it looks as though it is too thick to cut. Don't compromise your design for this reason alone.
2. Does it have scratches that will show up in the bevel? All plate glass must be checked for scratches before you start working with it, even when it comes to you straight from the glazer. In fact, glass of this kind can show the most scratches.
3. Mark off glass that is severely scratched for pencil bevels. So long as one surface is clear, the other surface doesn't matter. You will be removing it anyway.
4. Check to see if the glass is old or new. You can tell by looking at the edge. Old glass is greenish or yellowish on edge; new glass is bluish.
5. Make certain that the glass you choose will allow your pattern to fit its surface with plenty of overlap. It is a mistake to try to save glass at the expense of difficulty in cutting a particular

24

Fig. 2-1 A star pattern transferred to the glass blank. Always make sure that you leave enough glass around the whole pattern so that you can work comfortably.

shape. You will probably end up after considerable labor breaking the piece for lack of room to maneuver your score lines.

6. Hold the glass up to the light to make sure it doesn't have any hidden flaws. Some plate glass hides cracks or chips within its width. As you begin to score it, the pressure you apply can cause these flaws to crack the glass. You can get cut when this happens unexpectedly.

7. The glass should be absolutely clean. If it has a haze on it, clean it before cutting. Otherwise you may find that the haze won't come off, and you may have a perfectly cut but dirty— and therefore unusable—result. Your glass must be absolutely clean before you apply the cutter.

8. Check the glass for any sharp points or edges and remove these before starting to cut. Because of its thickness, plate glass can break unevenly, leaving small shards sticking out of the cut line. Don't disregard these; they may not disregard you.

Scoring Plate Glass

Scoring plate glass is done in the same manner as scoring any other type of glass. No, you don't have to exert more pressure because of the extra thickness of the piece. No, you don't have to have any particular kind of surface underneath. We have cut plate on bare wood, on newspaper padding, and on carpeting. It will break out of the score lines in the same manner regardless. What is important is that the undersurface be smooth and free from glass chips. Glass chips under your glass are a nemesis. No matter how many you brush away, others will appear. They will cut you and scratch your glass. Watch out for them, and check the glass often for new scratches that might have just been made

Fig. 2-2 Cutting plate. The upper surface of the glass has been broken away to follow the shape, and the pattern has been reapplied. The cutter is moved by pushing from the left-hand side of the pattern to the right. It could also be moved by pulling from the right to the left side of the pattern.

by these little devils. One of life's most frustrating moments is to finish up a beautiful bevel on the roughing wheel and discover a scratch right through it that you could swear was not there a minute ago. It was. You were just in too much of a hurry to see it.

So far as scratches go, some workers have a curious notion that they can be polished away without having any effect on the glass—as though the polishing wheels acted as big erasers. It is true that you can polish out superficial scratches on the felt wheel, but if you have a scratch in the glass that you can feel with your fingernail, forget it. To remove it, you will have to remove so much glass from the area to get below the scratch that you will end up with a distorted surface. In some instances, this distortion can be worse than the original scratch—and you will still have to throw the piece away.

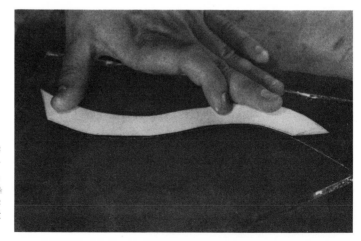

Fig. 2-3 Scoring the S shape. Note that the curve of the pattern is carried right to the edge of the glass, even though this portion won't be used. Continuing the curve to the edge makes it possible to break out the glass.

Fig. 2-4 The S-shape pattern being cut.

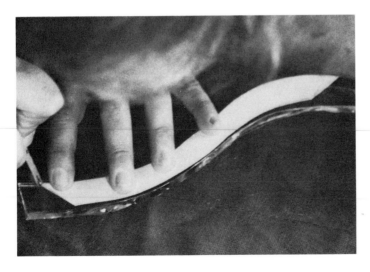

Fig. 2-5 Scoring the end of the S shape. Hold the pattern securely or the far end will drift off the glass.

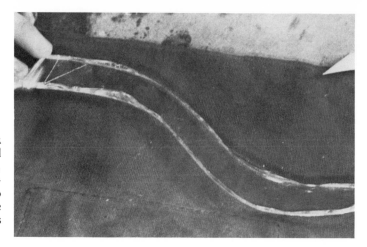

Fig. 2-6 The S-shape glass blank being cut. Note the straight and slanted lines that make the point. The straight line is broken out before the slanted line so as not to lose the point. Use the table edge and breaking pliers or the two-pliers technique for breaking out.

Just because your working surface is carpeted doesn't mean that you can be heedless about glass chips. Such sharp points will bury themselves in the pile of the carpet, to scratch viciously against your glass once you put cutting pressure upon it. The only way to guard against chips is to brush off your worktable surface frequently and thoroughly, no matter what material you have covered it with.

In scoring plate you may be an adherent of either the pushing school or the pulling school. Some workers like to pull the cutter toward them; others push it away. You might prefer to see where you are going rather than where you have been. If so, by all means remain a pusher. Some workers like to push the cutter on curves and pull it on long, straight lines.

What matters more than the direction in which you cut is whether you are using the proper cutter. A dull cutter that plows a wide angle through the surface of the thick plate will provide a more effective flaw to "run" than will a sharp cutter with its straighter cut line.

Rather than taking too many chances, use a cutter that is specifically made for scoring plate glass.

Breaking Out the Score

There are two standard methods for breaking out the score: the tapping method and breaking it out with pliers or fulcrum.

The Tapping Method

In tapping plate glass it is a good idea to turn it upside down on the surface of the table and smack fairly firmly over the score with the ball of your cutter. This is just the opposite of the method we advocate for tapping regular stained glass or tapping single- or double-strength window glass, where you hold the glass in your hand and tap from below. If you use this method with plate glass, you may get a sliver of glass in your eye because of the thickness.

Fig. 2-7 Cutting the pattern for a square. The glass-cutter wheel, placed flush against the pattern, is pulled toward the worker.

Fig. 2-8 Starting a score line with the pushing method. The line is continued from the bottom edge of the glass to the top (from the left to the right side in the picture).

Fig. 2-9 Scoring to pattern. A star pattern is placed on top of the glass and the cutter run along one surface. The glass is then turned over and tapped from the bottom.

Fig. 2-10 A nicely broken out score line in a piece of plate glass.

Also, you may not generate enough force by tapping from below to run the score to follow the score line. By having the glass on the table, the force of your tap is increased because of the firm surface underneath. Remember, the thicker the plate, the harder you have to tap. With thick plate, such as $\frac{3}{8}''$ or $\frac{1}{2}''$, you may not be able to use the ball of the cutter. You may have to substitute a dalle hammer, or at least a heavier tapper than the cutter handle.

The way you tap also affects the score line. As the score begins to *run* (that is, deepen), keep your taps directly in front of this deepening line. If you don't, the tap line will begin to vary from the score line. It may do this in any event; if so, give a sharp tap just in front of this deviation to bring the run back in line with the score. If you keep tapping in this manner, you should be able to run your score line right across the glass. Once this is accomplished, you will find it easy to separate the two pieces of glass by hand—if they haven't already fallen apart on the table.

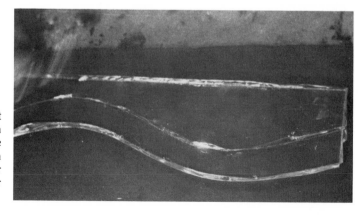

Fig. 2-11 The S shape, broken out at the bottom side, is tapped from the top at the upper portion. Note how nicely the score line has run the length of the shape. The tapper is still being applied at the upper left.

Fig. 2-12 Two large pieces of glass are separated at the score line. Note the extra glass allowed on the left and right sides of the star pattern. The glass should be broken evenly whenever possible so that you will have fewer odd pieces in your scrap pile.

There is a difference between breaking plate with pliers and breaking thinner glass. The most efficient way to score plate is to put the glass on the worktable and align the score line with the edge of the table. Grasp the excess glass with the pliers and pull. The pulling movement is mostly back and downward rather than the snapping motion used with thinner glass. (It's a good idea not to wear open-toed shoes during this procedure!)

Breaking with Pliers

Fig. 2-13 Tapping a score line from above the glass but below the score. The glass has been turned over and lies upside down on the table. This piece of glass would be much too awkward to hold and tap from below. A ball-end Fletcher cutter is shown.

This method usually brings out a certain timidity in some hobbyists. Because the glass is thick, it appears to be not only unworkable, but dangerous. Yet plate glass is actually softer than most double-strength glass, and it is far less brittle than single strength. In fact, once you get used to scoring and breaking plate, you may find it difficult to work with single-strength window glass.

As we have said, there is usually no problem in scoring and breaking $\frac{1}{4}''$ plate glass for anyone who has already worked in stained glass. But if you use $\frac{3}{8}''$ and $\frac{1}{2}''$ plate, it can be very threatening at first. To become experienced, you will have to practice and break a lot of glass. But perhaps more quickly than you might think, you will begin to find that working with any thickness becomes routine.

Remember that the reason for using thick plate is its ability to take steeper angles; thus your prisms will be more effective, and they will stand out dramatically from the background surface. One advantage of this is that on a large piece of glass—for a door, let's say—a narrow $\frac{1}{2}''$ bevel would get lost. Even if you had a 1" bevel on $\frac{1}{4}''$ plate, the angle would be so gradual and the demarcation so diffuse, that your eye might read it as a single plane and miss the bevel altogether.

Other Methods

We have already mentioned the Pittsburgh Plate running pliers. These will break out curved lines as well as long, straight lines. The only proviso here is that the curves will not be very acute. The pliers are used in the same way as you would use any running pliers: Line up the center of the jaws with the score line and press the handles together with a smoothly increasing force. The pliers are rugged and are meant to run scores on thick pieces of glass.

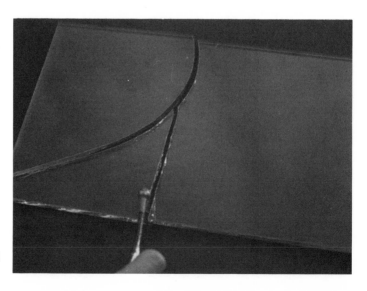

Fig. 2-14 Tapping the entire score line.

Fig. 2-15 Using fulcrums to break a score line. It is sometimes best, for long lines, to use fulcrums of different thicknesses. Here the back of a glass cutter is used as one breaking area, and a nail as the other. This minimizes the overall force that is applied and permits better control.

It is also possible to use a fulcrum beneath the score line in a piece of plate, provided the glass is not too thick to prevent enough force from being applied to run the score (see Fig. 2-15). And of course, if the glass is large enough, you can snap off a straight line by using the edge of the table.

Once you have decided on a particular shape, select your glass for it with care. Be sure to watch for good and bad sides. The glass is likely to chip on the underneath side when you break it with pliers for your rough outline. It also tends to chip on the side

Pattern-Cutting Plate

Fig. 2-16 Breaking pliers used with the table edge to break out the first inside curve of the star pattern.

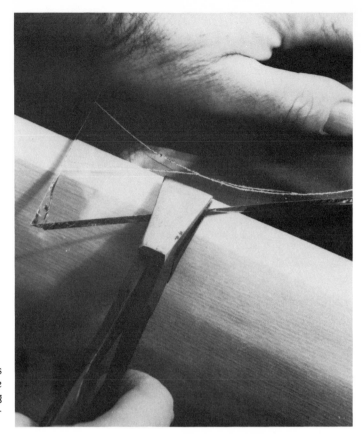

Fig. 2-17 Using breaking pliers. This is not a good area for using these pliers, since three lines are meeting and the strain on the glass is somewhat uncontrolled.

that you tap. Keeping this in mind, you can select a piece of glass that is already chipped on one side provided the other side is clean. Of course you must be able to fit your pattern into the workable surface, leaving enough room to work away the excess. Too many students work with plate the way they work with stained glass—they attempt to use every last crumb. Don't be afraid to waste plate. In the long run you'll save both glass and time.

If you select a piece of glass that is chipped on one side, it doesn't matter if the glass further chips on this side as you work. You will be beveling this side anyway. Chipping and flaking of the glass here means that you will have less surface to take off. Naturally you must stay on guard to prevent any chipping in the final piece. Obviously any chip that shows in the finished bevel is a disaster. And it is always possible that chipping will occur while you are getting the glass to shape on the side you will not be beveling. There is no rule that says all chipping will occur on the bad side. If you chip glass on the side to be beveled, don't waste time trying to fix the defect or attempt to convince yourself that

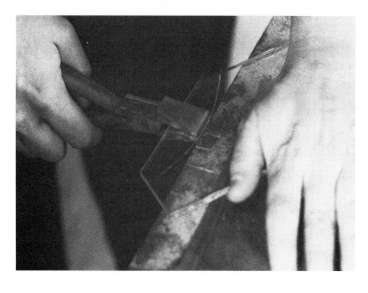

Fig. 2-18 Breaking plate. The score line is placed over the table edge and grasped firmly with the breaking pliers in a slightly downward pulling motion. Since this is an inside curve, the pliers are "jawed" at the center of the curve, which gives even pressure along the score line.

it isn't really there. Just throw the piece away and start again. There is nothing to be gained in beveling down the glass and being left with a chip that the lead won't cover. This will stand out like a sore thumb—one of yours, no doubt, obtained by beveling this very piece.

When pattern-cutting plate, we turn our patterns upside down against the worst of the two surfaces. This is the surface that we will then grozze or tap against, so it is the surface that we expect to be flawed.

Fig. 2-19 Pulling off the ends of an S shape. This can be somewhat difficult if you aren't careful. Inadequate scoring of the glass is a major source of breakage at these points. The breaking pliers should be placed right up to the score line. The force exerted on the pliers is more back than downward.

Fig. 2-20 Using running pliers. Step 1: The guide line on the jaw is lined up with the score line of an outside curve.

Fig. 2-21 Step 2: Pressure is applied with the pliers.

Fig. 2-22 Step 3: A clean break is achieved. Don't worry about breaking the entire curve at once. You can remove the remainder of the glass with breaking pliers or make another run with the running pliers.

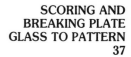

Fig. 2-23 To break the long score line at left, use running pliers or, as shown, the back of a glass cutter as a fulcrum.

When you are working with a pattern that is not symmetrical, you must know which side of the glass you will eventually bevel. Don't depend on memory alone. Invariably you will pick up the glass and bevel what you think is the correct side, only to discover too late that you beveled the wrong side. Glass has a mind of its own in this respect: It can turn on its back like a turtle as it waits to be beveled.

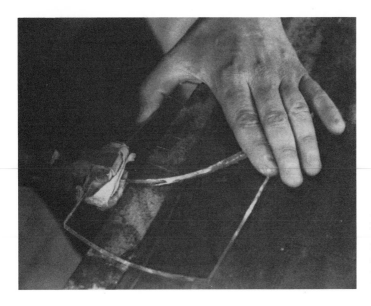

Fig. 2-24 Using running pliers to break out the score. When pressure is applied, the run line follows the score line directly. The glass is held flat with the edge extending slightly beyond the table.

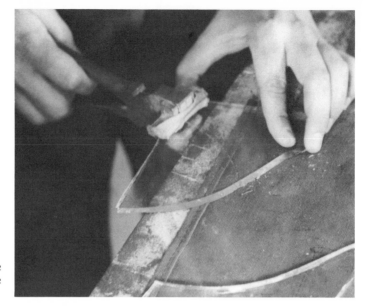

Fig. 2-25 Breaking out the top score line with running pliers. Note the smooth break that the pliers give.

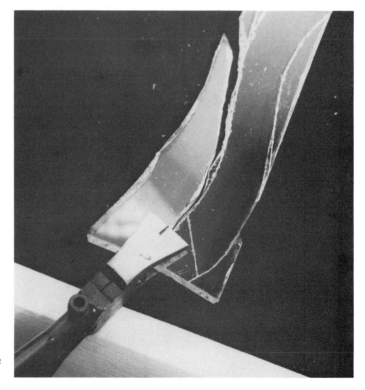

Fig. 2-26 Breaking out an S shape with regular running pliers.

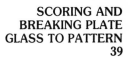

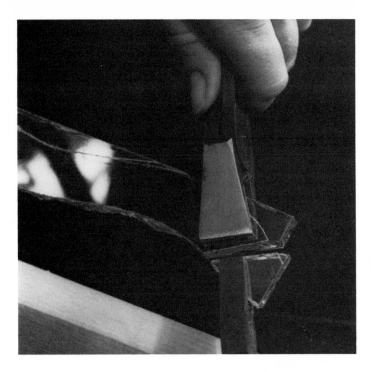

Fig. 2-27 The two-pliers technique helps to preserve the point of the S shape that will become a pencil bevel. The glass is held with the wider-jawed breaking pliers (top), and most of the force is applied with the small grozzing pliers (below).

Fig. 2-28 Using the two-pliers technique to separate pieces.

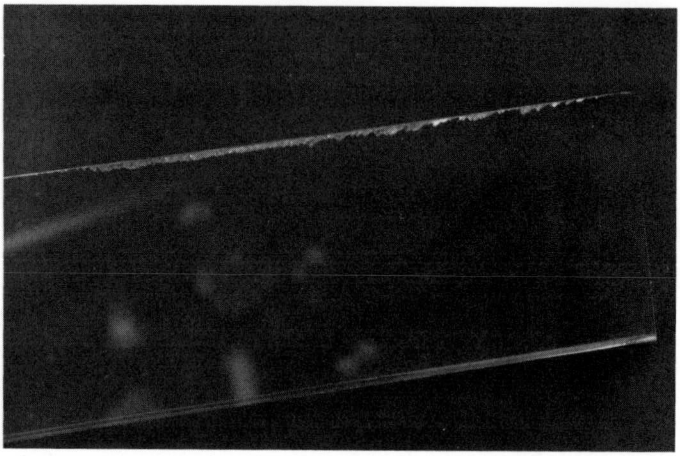

Fig. 2-29 Plate glass, because of its thickness, can chip along an edge after it is broken out. This is the surface that is used for the bevel.

It is a good idea to mark with a red pencil BTS (Bevel This Side). Or you can just make a cross on it. BTS is very specific, though, and it tells anyone you may be working with the precise message. An X or any other mark, even though it may be meaningful to you, may be ambiguous to someone else. Mark your paper pattern pieces the same way so that you can tell the up side at a glance. With the patterns marked, you can easily get into the habit of turning them upside down on the glass pieces so that you will never bevel on the wrong side.

Grozzing

One question always arises regarding grozzing: Do I have to start off with a perfectly cut piece of plate before I start to bevel? The answer is no. Some craftsmen who carry over stained-glass techniques into working with plate glass automatically assume that the piece of glass must be finely grozzed before the next step can be accomplished. But in working with plate, especially thick plate, this kind of hand-grozzing takes too much time and also can lead to fractures. Don't worry about hand-grozzing your plate. The first of the beveling wheels, the roughing wheel, is a terrific grozzer. You can even use it for grozzing your stained glass as well. It will do the job rapidly and effectively. It will also grozze your fingernails, so you will have to be extra careful. Actually, you will find that long fingernails and beveling do not go together. The nails always lose out.

If you are dealing with points in your glass pattern, you will have to take extra care when grozzing or breaking out. When breaking out a pointed score line, pull with the pliers from the point itself rather than from any area below it. This holds true especially when you are working with a long point. Pulling the score line at the point tends to preserve it; pulling from the middle of the score usually will destroy the point.

Inside and outside curves can be hand-grozzed if you are using $\frac{1}{4}''$ plate, but if the glass is thicker, these areas have to be broken out. Keep the curves gradual for an easier breakout. If your curves are too acute, you will probably lose them. Even the machine cannot grozze a steeply angled inside curve. Running pliers, of course, can be used on outside curves.

Remember: Don't try to save plate by squeezing the score line on the edges. Make sure that you have enough excess glass on each side of the score line so that you can break out the score effectively.

If you have a very fine point in a bevel, especially in thick plate, but even in $\frac{1}{4}''$ plate, don't try to grozze with the running pliers. Even the two-pliers technique—grasping the glass within the score line with one pair and the excess with the other—will probably destroy the point.

The easiest way to keep the point is to grozze with the roughing wheel of the beveling machine. If your glass edges are ragged, clean them up on the machine.

Care of the Patterns

Beveling involves using a lot of water, and water can lead to a mess if it is not kept under control. Your hands will probably be wet most of the time. You will have to keep wiping water off your glass as it is being beveled in order to see the bevel. You will also have to wipe your glasses over and over again. In no instance, however, can water wreak greater havoc than on your paper patterns. At the least, they will become limp, providing anything but the rigid borders that are required of a pattern. At the worst, they may swell and distort, giving you a false shape as a guide. If they get too soaked, they will turn into pulp, and you will have to make the whole pattern over again.

The best way to keep your patterns dry is to keep them away from the beveling machine. There is little enough reason for them to be there anyway. Keep the patterns on a table nearby. When you check your glass against the pattern, take the glass to the table rather than bringing the pattern to the beveling machine.

Glass Grinders

A number of companies make units for glass grinding (see our book, *Crafting in Glass* for a detailed discussion of the equipment). These machines are extremely useful in stained glass to achieve all sorts of intricate shapes that are out of the range of simple hand-cutting. Any of these machines can be used as an adjunct to your beveling machine, especially when it comes to producing inside curves.

At the same time, if you don't have a glass grinder, it isn't necessary to buy one specifically for beveling. You should be able to produce fine inside curves by hand and by learning to use the beveling machine.

If you have already been working in stained glass and you have a grinder, here is a word of warning: Be careful. Don't rely entirely

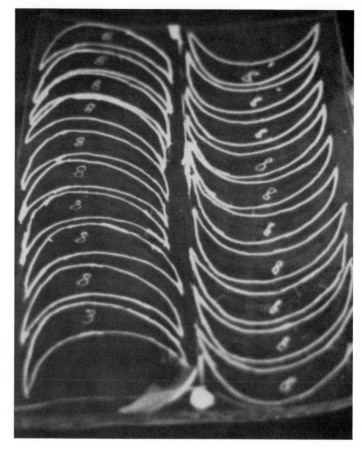

Fig. 2-30 These pieces were marked directly on the glass, since this ⅜″ plate glass was already curved for the project at hand. A glass bandsaw was used to cut them out; you could not cut these by hand. To save glass, the pieces were drawn as close together as possible. (Courtesy PRISM Glass.)

on the grinder to do your work for you. Learn to use your glass cutter as well. With the glass cutter and your beveler, you will be well on your way.

We have seen craftsmen produce very intricate shapes with their grinders and then bevel them on their beveling machines. Another caution, however: Not all of these queerly cut pieces can be beveled. During the beveling process, stresses and strains are created in the glass, and they could easily lead to fractures in the piece. That is time wasted. Where the grinder can help is in routine shaping of many similar pieces. Cutting these by hand can be a tedious process, and it will teach you nothing—except that it might be a good idea to purchase a grinder.

Slat Racks

Glass that is left lying flat on the table is subject to various evil influences. For one thing, pieces of glass tend to slip off tables. For another, they tend to pile up, one on another, even if you have been careful to prevent this. Small pieces can get lost amid

Fig. 2-31 A slat rack containing various glass blanks to be used in an upcoming project. This arrangement makes it easy to pick out the pieces, and it prevents them from being scratched.

Fig. 2-32 A slat rack holding roughed glass. The back pieces await their turn.

working debris. Wet glass makes a mess when it is laid flat. Pieces of glass scattered on a table surface are difficult to sort out. Even if you think you know where a certain piece of glass is, you probably won't be able to find it when you want it. If you are going to become involved with any project that will contain more than five or six pieces, it would be worth your while to build a slat rack.

A slat rack is a simple wooden frame designed to keep the glass pieces standing up and separate from one another. Slat racks have many advantages. In addition to preventing scratches on the glass, they allow you to catalogue all your work pieces or locate different sections of one project at a glance. A rack lets you see what has been done and how much is yet to do. In short, the slat rack can be a computer as well as a repository.

At the beginning of any multiple-piece project, cut out all the pieces and stand them in the rack. Then rough each piece and put it back in the rack. We do this routine through all the stages of the polishing. When we are finished, we have a slat rack full of (we hope) perfect bevels just waiting to be taken out of the rack and assembled. Slat racks are extremely helpful in large studios where many jobs are being done at the same time. Here the racks prevent confusing the pieces of one job with another, especially when people are working in particularly tight quarters.

CHAPTER 3

General Principles of Glass Beveling

This chapter is an actual beveling course. When you have completed the "course," you will be able to apply your artistry to what you have learned and begin to express your individuality in glass. Beveling is a creative art as well as a craft, and it can be a powerful one. Even if you have already learned something about the beveling process, assume that you have never beveled a piece of glass, that the process is more or less a mystery to you, and that you have not established any particular prejudices for or against any specific machine. If you are just starting out, so much the better. Sign up for this course, and as Steve Williams says in the Prologue, "begin."

A Few Hints on Procedures

1. We will begin with straight-line beveling and go on to inside curves, outside curves, and S curves. These are the four basic shapes in beveling. Doing outside curves, which includes circles and ovals, is the most difficult procedure. The S-curve demonstration is a lesson in making pencil bevels. A pencil bevel is one where the complete surface of the glass becomes beveled.

There is no flat surface on an S-shape pencil bevel. With any other bevel you will have a flat surface of glass with perhaps $\frac{1}{2}''$ bevels running all around the edges. A pencil bevel may be 1" or less wide per piece with two bevels on it. Thus there will be no untouched surface of glass. The central edge gives the "pencil" ridge.

Note that a pencil bevel is not limited to an S shape; any configuration that reverses from an inside to an outside curve in one continuous flow may be referred to as an S curve (*not* an S shape), including a paisley or comma design, for one.

2. Other techniques that can be done with the beveling machine include glass engraving and "brilliant work." Working with mirror opens up an entirely new galaxy of effects using the same techniques that apply to clear glass. All of these effects can be

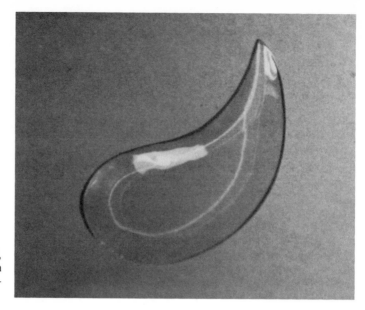

Fig. 3-1 The paisley-shaped bevel, like the S shape, reverts from an inside to an outside curve in a single continuous line.

combined with any type of beveled piece. For instance, often pencil bevels are notched. This technique started in the Victorian era, the golden age of beveling. Many beveled windows were notched, although the process is not so prevalent today. These techniques are called "brilliant work" because they enhance the reflectability—hence the brilliance—of the glass by increasing the number of facets on its surface. They are also called "bright work."

3. Because we will use different thicknesses of glass, you should stock up on plate varying from $\frac{1}{4}''$ thick on up. Try to get some old plate as well as new. Most of this glass can be obtained as scrap from your local glazier. Plate glass is one material where you can save yourself a lot of money, unlike stained glass.

Also try to get some scrap pieces of flashed stained glass. When you bevel this material, you get an edge of one color and a flat surface of another. It can be very dramatic. When we make notched pencil bevels, we usually use $\frac{3}{8}''$ plate. This allows the bevel and the notching to stand forth without looking crowded. However, you may prefer an even thicker plate than this.

The Four Basic Steps

4. There are four basic steps in beveling, although we occasionally use five if we are using all vertical wheels. The steps are divided into the different wheels, or "stations," that are employed: roughing, smoothing, semipolishing, and polishing. Each step has its own problems and defects. All of these defects are correctable up to a point. That point is reached once you have removed so

much glass that you no longer have the room to make the correction. Then distortion enters the picture. One major problem—and perhaps the most frustrating—is faceting, or "waves" that appear within the surface of the bevel. These are caused by uneven smoothing on the second step, the smoothing stone.

5. Of all the beveling shapes, the S shape is the most difficult for most people to cut the blank for. A hint may be helpful: After scoring, turn the blank upside down on the worktable and tap over the score. Start to tap on the inside curve of the S, because that's where you will lose it if you are going to lose it. Tap slightly in front of where the score runs so that it won't have the tendency to run off the line. On the ends of the score, where the glass is weakest, support the glass with your whole hand. Warning: These end cuts are very deceptive. By this time you have the whole shape almost out. What can possibly go wrong? Then you pull or tap or cut the wrong way at the end and the whole piece shatters. It takes patience and practice to make S shapes from plate.

Equipment and Cautions

6. Beveling is a messy operation, so wear work clothes, use an apron, and don't set up your machine in the kitchen or living room. You will need a water line, which can come either from the basement sink or from outside. If you are working in a garage, you could even use a garden hose.

Use a drip bucket to catch excess water as it flows out of the machine. Drain or throw the water outside. Don't dump the water down the drain because the grit may clog it. And don't put this excess water on your plants because the compounds may harm them.

Keep children away from the beveling machine; children have a way of making any machine dangerous. The same holds true for the beveling compounds. They are not toxic, but if misused they can lead to problems.

You and the Machine

7. It is up to you whether or not you clean your beveling machine after using it. Most bevelers leave their machines alone until the buildup of debris becomes an obstacle to their work. In any event, before you clean the machine the compounds must dry.

8. Your relationship to your machine is a purely personal one. It doesn't matter if you sit, stand, or do both as you bevel. You should make yourself as comfortable as possible. Remember, beveling is a slow process—you are not running a race. You will learn as you go, training your eye and getting a feel for the procedure. There is no one way to hold the glass against any of the wheels, although we may sound on occasion as though there is. Some techniques work better than others in this regard. Of course you can devise your own technique—whatever you decide will give you the best results.

Fingernails are a problem because there is just no way to protect them. You can't wear gloves because they will rip. Rubber fingertips may protect the fingers when you are beveling large to medium pieces of glass, but when it comes to beveling small pieces, it is especially difficult to protect the fingers, and especially the nails. Your skin is safe, although if you insist on working with tiny pieces of glass hour after hour, you will probably end up with some abrasions on your fingers as well as beveling your nails. This is a problem that you will have to come to terms with.

9. As you bevel, learn to look at your glass in different kinds of light. Natural light—daylight—is best, but you should also look at it in artificial light. This helps you to detect flaws, especially facets. One kind of light will show a flaw that another kind didn't. Move the glass around as you look through it. Facets may show up only when the piece is moved and the light plays on them. If the bevel is not polished properly, reflected light may show this best. Under direct light the bevel may look perfect. It can fool you.

10. You may be able to use your beveling machine (check with the manufacturer) for materials other than glass. You might use it to polish metal or stones or any material that will be amenable to the speed of the wheels. Beveling machines are quite adaptable, and it is fun to wander out of the realm of glass and poke your nose into another craft from time to time.

Beveling Terminology

Beveling terminology is fairly specific, but it can be confusing since different people mean different things by the same terms. In most instances, the confusion lies with the term *bevel* itself. We use the word *bevel* for the entire piece of glass, the edges of which have been slanted at less than a 95-degree angle with the existing surface, or, as in pencil bevels, with the remaining surface edge. We also use the term for the particular slanted edge itself so far as its length is concerned.

We use the term *mitre* for the width of the bevel. If you hold a beveled piece of glass directly in front of you, the bevel runs from left to right, whereas the mitre runs up and down.

The *angle* is the line made by the mitre with the untouched glass surface. It is also the line between contiguous bevels. The mitre controls the angle. Thus the bevel is the mitre plus the angles—in short, the entire piece of glass.

If you understand these three terms, you will have little difficulty following this book or talking with another beveler.

The following terms in the beveler's vocabulary are also essential.

Roughing wheel or station. The first wheel that is used to get the glass shape. It may be a cast-iron, steel, or diamond wheel.

Smoothing wheel. The second wheel used in beveling. It can be a "natural" wheel—such as a Newcastle sandstone—or an artificial one, such as aluminum oxide or cast iron.

Cork wheel. The third wheel used in beveling. A solid cork wheel used with pumice for polishing.

Fiber wheel. The polishing wheel in a vertical machine.

Felt wheel. The final wheel, used with jeweler's rouge or cerium oxide to give the perfect finish to the bevel.

Scalloping (or, actually, gouging). An effect that results from allowing the glass to remain too long in one spot on the roughing wheel or on the smoothing stone.

Tapering. Where a bevel starts at one width and ends at another, diminishing in some instances to a fine line.

Step bevel. The process of beveling within a bevel, giving the effect of steps going down to the edge. This is actually step-mitring, but both terms are used.

Cross bevel. Where a bevel changes direction within its plane; that is, it angles in a slightly different direction from the beginning of the bevel.

Notched bevel. A bevel in which the angle has been worked with an engraving wheel to make discrete scallops. The scallops can be spaced or contiguous, giving a beaded effect.

Diminishing bevel. Instead of running the length of the glass edge, the bevel fades into the surface partway down. It is a planned process of not completing the line of the beveled edge.

Vertical wheels. Wheels that turn from a straight up-and-down position. The worker uses the rim of the wheel.

Horizontal wheels. Wheels that lie flat; the worker uses the wide surface.

Flaws and Frustrations

Facets (Waves)

Facets, or waves, are multiple small surfaces within the area of the bevel. They are mostly caused by the smoothing stone, the second step in the beveling process, and they are mostly removed by the smoothing stone as well. They can be difficult to remove, and many workers will try to remove the more obvious ones while letting the rest go. Some workers will leave the facets in the bevel as an example of "human" versus machine craftsmanship. We feel this is a contradiction in terms, or, more likely, an excuse for laziness. Because facets break up the even flow of light through the bevel and are disconcerting, giving the effect of poor workmanship, they should be removed. It is of course a question of degree and comparison.

To the untrained eye, the facets in a beveled window look wonderful. Yet, if you place this window next to one where the bevels are more even and true, the improved aesthetic effect is apparent at once. Here you will see the nonfaceted bevels breaking up the light more evenly, providing almost a measured rather than a fragmented and confused prism effect. Even on reflected light, the glisten of the more perfect bevels will show more strongly.

The Defect Bevel

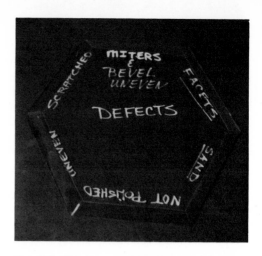

Fig. 3-2 This is a good teaching and learning example.

Fig. 3-3 A haze or cloudiness covers the area that has not been adequately polished.

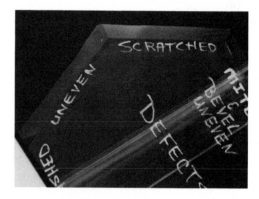

Fig. 3-4 Note how the scratches—two on the right and a smaller one on the left—stand out. Also shown are uneven mitre angles. Compared to the angle of the glass edge, the one on the left of the scratched surface is considerably off.

Fig. 3-5 Note the facets—the wavy lines and areas of light and shadow—on the surface.

Fig. 3-6 Note the small grains of sand peppered throughout the surface of the bevel.

The rainbow in the more perfect window will be stronger than the less perfect, and the colors will be more effective.

The term *faceted bevel* describes the end result of beveling, meaning that the facets have been imposed upon what was previously a flat surface. What you see are waves, an unevenly mitred surface. Although this may be fine in a diamond, in beveling it is a defect. Facets provide high and low ridges. When the light travels through them, it is broken up irregularly and becomes diffused. It spreads in so many different directions that it produces a color less intense than that of a nonfaceted bevel. In other words, a proper bevel will show a more intense rainbow than an improper one. Save the facets for your diamonds, which shine strictly by reflecting light. Beveled glass, on the other hand, shines from reflected light and imposes its character by refracted light.

Sand

In the South they call sand "snow." Sand is the gritty surface that is left on the entire bevel after roughing, the first step in the process. All of the sand must be removed in succeeding steps, right down to the very last grain. Otherwise it will leave obvious flaws in the bevel and will mark the worker as a poor one indeed. Most of the sand, if not all of it, is properly removed in smoothing, at the second step in the beveling process. If you have sand in the bevel after this step, it means that you either have not worked long enough at the smoothing stone or you are not working at it properly. Unfortunately, it is the smoothing stone that also makes facets, so you may be adding these while getting rid of the sand. However, it's an unfair world, and you can cheer yourself up with the knowledge that you are establishing a good technique.

Keep in mind that each step in the beveling process, each wheel, removes traces of the wheel before. With the smoothing stone, you are removing the side effects of the cast-iron roughing wheel. Obviously you are removing glass at the same time. There is a balance between the amount of glass you can remove and the amount of surface that remains flawed. This becomes particularly important when dealing with scratches. Removing sand is fairly routine. If you will do your best to get rid of all the sand on the second wheel, you will be through with the job. If not, you will have to go back to the smoothing wheel *after* the cork wheel when you see the little mountains of sand in the polished surface of the bevel. You may have to wiggle the glass a bit as you hold it up to the light to make certain all the sand is gone.

Scratches

Even if you see no scratches when you pick up your glass, you may find you missed at least one when you look at it again in a highly reflective light. Don't congratulate yourself too soon! The glass can still be scratched during use.

Scratches are often caused by the smoothing stone. This comes about either because the smoothing stone is being run too dry, or it has become contaminated with the silicon carbide from the roughing station. Try to guard against this. It seems that this should be simple to prevent, but it happens more often than one would like. Keep your stations free from the beveling compounds, and always make sure you have enough water on the smoothing stone. Scratches also occur from natural (Newcastle) sandstone, which may contain many impurities.

Cloudy Bevel

A bevel that is not polished sufficiently will be cloudy when you hold it up to the light. A finished bevel should be sparkling clear. If your bevel is cloudy, you must go back and repolish. The fault lies somewhere in this process: Either you have used the wrong polishing materials, the wrong wheel, the wrong speed, or you have not given enough time to the procedure. The fault is not, as some students like to think, in the glass. A cloudy bevel is a common mistake.

Uneven Bevel

In an uneven bevel the mitres are uneven in width. In other words, you start out at one width and you end up with another. This is an extremely disconcerting experience, especially if you have not been checking your bevel constantly and are happily going along thinking that all is well. What you have to do here, obviously, is straighten out the bevel. But this is often easier said than done. Now you must proceed slowly. If you attempt to straighten out the bevel in one swoop, you may overcompensate and find your ridge going the other way. You may end up with a pencil bevel on a piece of glass that was originally 6″ across. It is better to go slowly, a little at a time, when you try to fix any errors.

Mismatched Mitre Angles

Mitred angles should go directly into the corners of the glass. When they do not, your work will appear amateurish and sloppy. The mitred angles can be thrown off as the first occurrence in a number of steps in the beveling process. The problem is compounded when you fail to keep checking the width of the bevel from the top line to the edge of the glass—in other words, the measurement of the mitred portion. This should be checked at several points along the line. If you keep a check on the glass edge, you can automatically check the angle of the mitre. The edge of the glass will tell you all you need to know. If the edge is thinner in one place than in another, you know you have to remove more glass to make the surface even. When you do this, the angle (mitre) has to come out right.

Bowing of the Mitre

Bowing of the mitre is also a smoothing-stone problem. It is mainly the result of either too much pressure on one part of the glass against the stone or uneven pressure, or the glass was left too long in one area of the stone. Usually the mitre tends to bow in the center because many workers seem to concentrate more on the ends of the bevel, assuming that these are the areas where they will have trouble. This defect is readily correctable. Just do

Somewhere Under the Rainbow. Anita Isenberg. 21″ x 11″.

Rocks and Waves. Anita Isenberg. 10½″ x 21″.

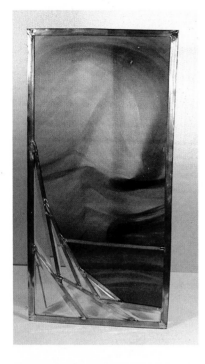

Beveled butterfly. Seymour Isenberg. 12″ x 6″.

Bevels Going to Pot. Anita Isenberg. 15″ x 25″.

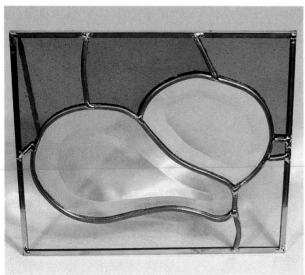

Still life. Anita Isenberg. 21″ wide.

Beveled lampshade. Barbara Basham. Photograph by Brian Patarich.

Divider panel for physician's office. Barbara Basham. 8' long. Photograph by Brian Patarich.

Cornucopia. Barbara Basham. 3' long, ranging from 12″ to 24″ in depth. Photograph by Brian Patarich.

Portrait panel.
Barbara Basham.
30″ deep.
Photograph by
Brian Patarich.

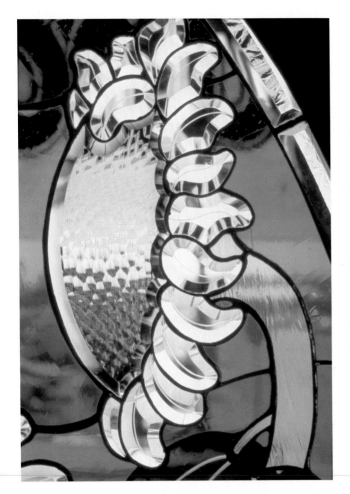

Detail, *Sunflower*. Barbara Basham. Photograph by Brian Patarich.

Beveled shield. Barbara Basham.
Photograph by Brian Patarich.

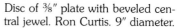
Disc of ⅜″ plate with beveled central jewel. Ron Curtis. 9″ diameter.

Detail of engraved disc. Ron Curtis. 12″ diameter.

Circular panel combining clear bevels and antique stained glass. Ron Curtis. 12″ diameter.

Detail of traditional bevel cluster from an arch window. Ron Curtis.

Dish-shaped disc from ⅜″ plate. Ron Curtis. 9″ diameter.

Dome made of 5,500 pieces of glass, half of them beveled. Steve Williams. 16′ diameter; 23″ drop; weighs three-quarters of a ton. Colored glass made by Uroborous Glass, Portland, Oregon.

Beveled and stained glass skylight. Steve Williams. Owned by Mr. and Mrs. Robert Redford. 15′ x 5′.

Window combining bevels and stained glass. Mark Bogenrief. Photograph by the artist.

Lettered window. Mark Bogenrief. Photograph by the artist.

Detail from a beveled window showing beaded work. Mark Bogenrief. Photograph by the artist.

Arch of beveled and stained glass. Mark Bogenrief. 7'2" x 8'2". Photograph by the artist.

Three-piece set. Mark Bogenrief. 7' x 4½'. Photograph by the artist.

A jewel-like window. Mark Bogenrief. 3' x 6'. Photograph by the artist.

Prototype panel showing the use of colored bevels. Allen H. Graef. Photograph by the artist.

Detail from beveled *fleur de lis* panel. A traditional design with a contemporary approach, utilizing beveled ''peak rounds,'' ⅜″ thick. Allen H. Graef. Photograph by the artist.

Door panel. Allen H. Graef. Owned by Hunt Farms, Merced, California. Photograph by Mrs. Hunt.

A prototype panel of thick dimensional shapes, available from The Glass Bevel. This panel displays some of the shapes and is free-floating within a brass frame. Allen H. Graef. Photograph by the artist.

Panel of clear and colored bevels. Allen H. Graef. 18″ x 22″. Photograph by the artist.

Gas Bladders. Colored bevels and thick "peaked rounds." Designed by Sue Youry for The Glass Bevel. Located in the Sigler residence, South Laguna Beach, California. 2′ x 8′. Photograph by Bill Jessee.

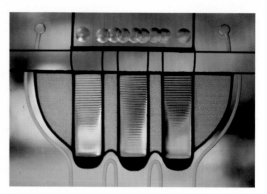

Detail, *Exercise #8*. Sandblasted, acid etched, with microscope slides. Carl Powell, copyright © 1978.

Exercise #51. Black glass, German flashed white on clear beveled glass, frenel lenses. Carl Powell, copyright © 1981. 23″ x 26″.

Detail, *Exercise #51*.

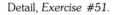

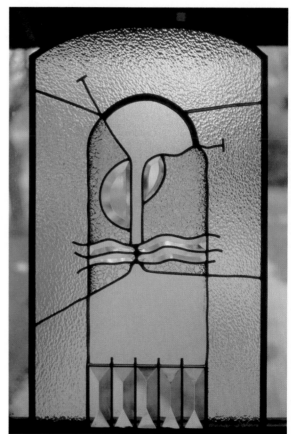

Untitled; WWII tank periscope prisms, beveled, at bottom of panel. Carl Powell, copyright © 1980. 21″ x 36″.

Exercise #21. Carl Powell, copyright © 1979. 28½″ x 34½″.

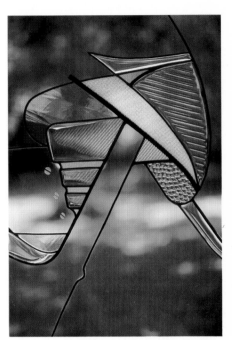

Exercise #17. Beveled refrigerator shelves, double glazed. Carl Powell, copyright © 1979. 33½″ x 24½″.

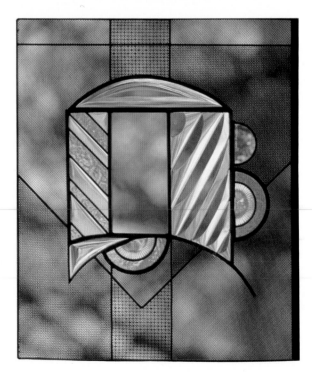

Exercise #19. Wineglass bottoms, screen background, zinc and steel. Carl Powell, copyright © 1979. 21″ x 25″.

Exercise #27. Beveled, fluted glass and acid-etched bubbles. Carl Powell, copyright © 1980. 25½″ x 20″.

Exercise #41. Carl Powell, copyright © 1981. 16½″ x 13½″.

Exercise #23. Carl Powell, copyright © 1979. 27″ x 33½″.

Exercise #43. Carl Powell, copyright © 1981. 16½″ x 13½″.

Fig. 3-7 Machine-made bevels. Note how many of the corner mitred angles do not match up to the glass angles.

more smoothing in the center than on the ends for awhile. Unless the mitre is radically off, this will usually straighten it out.

Machine Bevels Versus Hand Bevels

Since we are discussing crooked mitres and other human flaws, it is interesting to think that machines, not being human, would make perfect bevels. And, indeed, some people look at crooked mitres and think they are better than straight mitres since (as with leaving in the facets) they are a sure sign that the piece was crafted by hand. Actually machines mostly tend to make poor mitres. By hand, you are more likely to come out with a straight mitre. Why? Mainly because the machine heads must be constantly adjusted to attain this height of perfection. And the truth is that, more often than not, such constant tinkering with the machine provides more downtime than the bevel manufacturer can afford. So inferior bevels are often passed by many manufacturers. The logic seems to be that the inferior bevels will appear to have been produced by hand because of their very defects. It's more than a little unfair when you think about it.

The Perfect Bevel

What is a perfect bevel? No one we have ever asked claims to have ever seen one. It is an ideal that seems to be forever beyond those of us who work in the craft. Theoretically, the perfect bevel would be as clear and undistorted as the entire surface of the untouched glass. This is a steep order, especially since in beveling the first thing you do is to deface the very same piece of glass that you then want to make perfectly natural again.

Beveling therefore is defacing, and defacing is basically a terminal process. The best that any beveler can hope for is to get back as close as possible to the original surface. This means absolutely perfect clarity. Since this is impossible, it is no wonder that the perfect bevel is so elusive. Only an experienced beveler can tell how close to perfect your bevel may be.

But forget about making it perfect. Instead, concentrate on making it as perfect as you can. Remove all flaws that you can see and apply a high polish. Don't depend for your plaudits on people who wouldn't know a good bevel from a bad one. If you do this, you will never improve your work. In fact, it may become worse and worse. When you want an opinion on your work, take it to someone who knows what beveling is all about. Only then will you get closer and closer to making the perfect bevel.

The Importance of Edge Thickness

The thickness of the beveled edge is a very important consideration. If the edge is too thin or too thick, it will crumble or throw the mitre out of line. As you are working, you can use this edge as a measure. The edge thickness should be between $\frac{1}{8}''$ to $\frac{1}{16}''$. If the edge is much thicker than $\frac{1}{8}''$, the mitre will be too slight. If the edge is much thinner than $\frac{1}{16}''$, the mitre will be weak and tend to crumble during polishing or assembly. What you want is the steepest mitre possible, one that will stand up throughout each station in the process.

One way *not* to check the edge is to run your finger along it. Some people are inveterate edge runners, and some people get cut. Even though a beveled edge usually will not cut, some do upon occasion. Besides, it is a bad habit to run your fingers over *any* glass edge.

Once your eye becomes trained to the task, it will readily tell you what the right width of your bevel is. It can easily be seen from the edge thickness. Until you develop this sense, use a small wooden ruler. We use a piece of broken stretch ruler, which works fine. Eventually your eye will quickly grasp the dimension of the mitre on its own, adding the edge thickness and the space of the bevel to compute the width. The human eye is an extremely accurate gauge.

When you do measure the width of your bevel, measure from behind the glass along the horizontal plane, not down the mitred portion. In other words, don't hold your ruler against the slope. Look through the glass at the ruler.

Growing Pains

Bevels, especially in the hands of beginners, tend to grow in width as glass is removed on each wheel. The bevel width may be $\frac{1}{2}''$ after roughing and, while that may be the width you want, it may end up $\frac{5}{8}''$ or even wider after smoothing. Remember that each wheel is removing glass, even the very finest polishing wheel. Polishing is not quite the same as erasing. Too often the beginner will consider it the same. When erasing, you are removing one material from another. In polishing, you are removing some of the original material to get to a better surface. Even in polishing ever so slightly, you are removing glass. Keeping this "growth" problem in mind, especially from the roughing through the smoothing stations, the best way we know to handle it is the "stop shy" method. For instance, if you find your bevel widen from $\frac{1}{2}''$ to $\frac{5}{8}''$ after using the smoothing stone, try stopping shy of your $\frac{1}{2}''$ desired width by $\frac{1}{8}''$ on the roughing wheel. By doing this you will allow for that much growth on the smoothing stone. You may have to stop shy by more than this, depending on your tendency to have your bevels grow in width. With practice, however, you will develop a smooth technique and will be able to cut your stop-shy margin down to $\frac{1}{32}''$ or even $\frac{1}{16}''$.

Your bevel can, of course, grow on the polishing wheels as well, but the amount would be so marginal that a micrometer would have to be employed to see it. Since the eye would not, it is not worth considering. You would more likely soften your bevel on these wheels than widen it. That's another problem.

We have been asked many questions about the beveling procedure. Some we reiterate here but with a different emphasis. Questions are all part of the learning process, and these provide a good review.

Q: Couldn't a guide or jig be set up to help me hold my glass at the correct angle?

A: After some hours of practice, you will find that a jig is useless. Your eye is your best guide. A jig has to be preset for each different-size bevel. This takes precious time, and it also can just get in your way. Bevelers for years have trained their hands and eyes to develop a "feel" for beveling without using time-consuming mechanisms such as jigs.

Q: Does it matter in which direction the beveling wheels turn?

A: It depends on your preference. Because beveling can be messy, you might find the wheels turning *away* from you help make it less so. Also with the wheels turning away, there is less drag on your arms. If you prefer to have the wheels turning toward you (a matter of comfort), you just have to reverse the polarity of the motor by changing the wires running from the motor to the shaft.

Q: What type of lighting is best for a beveling room?

A: Natural lighting is always best. However, an overhead fluorescent will work fine.

Q: Are there any tricks that will help my speed?

A: If you have several bevels to do, rough all of them, smooth all of them, and so on. This will pick up your speed tremendously. Also, just knowing what to expect from each wheel and training your eye to spot defects quickly will help.

Q: How long will the wheels last?

A: We have no statistics to go by, but we haven't worn out a wheel yet on the Denver machines. With proper use and care, you should get hundreds of hours of use from your wheels.

A Few Questions and Answers

Q: How often should I clean my machine?

A: There are no set rules. Your spray heads could become corroded and not function at their best. Or a problem could arise if too much glass ash and cerium oxide accumulates in the pan. This could clog your drain.

Q: Can I reuse the cerium oxide that is in the bottom pan of the machine?

A: Cerium oxide is a very fine polishing powder, and anything that contaminates it could reduce its efficiency. The white powder in the bottom pan of the machine is glass ash. If this gets into the cerium oxide mixture, it could scratch your bevel. Also, if you have used pumice on a cork wheel, the pumice residue would contaminate the cerium oxide. It is always best to use a fresh supply of cerium oxide.

Q: How much water should I have spraying on the wheels?

A: The spray heads in the Denver Machines are designed to spray as wide as the wheel. If the force of water is too great, the mist from the faucet will be wider than your wheel; it will spin off the nut or flange and give you a bath. On the other hand, if the spray is not strong enough, only part of your wheel will be wet.

Q: How often will the wheels need to be dressed?

A: If a very light touch is used continuously on the diamond wheel, it will need to be dressed often. The softer wheels, the fiber and the felt, also need to be dressed often. Every time a wheel is dressed, its size is reduced. As the fiber or felt wheels become smaller after many dressings, they can be used to make smaller bevels. We explain how to dress wheels in Chapter 5.

CHAPTER 4

The Beveling Process Begins: Roughing

We will use two of the Denver Glass Machinery beveling machines as models. This is an arbitrary choice, based on our familiarity with these machines, for they are our own. Also we feel that they are, in many ways, prototypes. Certainly the beveling procedure can be done on any other beveling machine as well. We favor the 4-in-1 compact design of the Denver units. You are of course free to choose for yourself when it comes to renting or purchasing a machine.

The two machines we will be demonstrating with are the Denver IB–16 and the Studio Model Beveler.

The IB–16 is meant for both professional and beginning bevelers. It is a ruggedly built, compact (38″ × 37″) beveling machine for the professional studio, capable of producing perfect bevels of any size and width. It includes two one-horsepower energy-efficient 220-volt Baldo industrial motors, safety switches with overload protection, large $2\frac{1}{4}″$ castors, and a stainless-steel grain chute. The machine is completely plumbed with spray heads. It has a heavy 2′ × 2′ square steel frame, four work lights, a 16″ × $1\frac{1}{2}″$ cast-iron roughing mill, a 16″ × 3″ cork wheel for polishing, and a 16″ × 3″ solid felt buffing wheel. This machine also has a high-speed two-spindle arbor for roughing and smoothing inside curves.

The high-speed arbor is essential unless you already own the Studio Model. The IB–16 comes without this feature at a slightly lower price. The high-speed wheels are the two outside ones. The inside wheels rotate at a lower speed than the outside ones. Because all of these wheels are vertical, we have the large wheels, the inside cork and felt wheels, rotating more slowly than the outer diamond and aluminum oxide ones, which are smaller; these are 6″ in diameter as opposed to 16″ for the cork and felt wheels.

This machine was not designed for the average hobbyist who just wants to turn out a beveled piece now and then. If you are

Two from Denver

57

Fig. 4-1A Denver Glass IB–16, showing the two horizontal stations. At right, the cast-iron grinding wheel; at left, the smoothing stone.

not fully committed to beveling, you would be better off with the Studio Model.

The Studio Model Beveler includes a ruggedly built arbor, an oversized cap start 110 volt, a $\frac{1}{3}$ horsepower motor, lifetime-sealed roller bearings, a stainless-steel shaft, a high-impact ABS base, flanges, nuts, and the highest quality knife-edge sprayers. It is also fully plumbed with standard hose connector and drain hose. This machine comes with all the wheels necessary to bevel. All the wheels are vertical; there are no horizontal wheels as on the IB–16, which uses a 16″ cast-iron wheel for roughing and the same

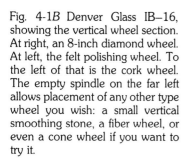

Fig. 4-1B Denver Glass IB–16, showing the vertical wheel section. At right, an 8-inch diamond wheel. At left, the felt polishing wheel. To the left of that is the cork wheel. The empty spindle on the far left allows placement of any other type wheel you wish: a small vertical smoothing stone, a fiber wheel, or even a cone wheel if you want to try it.

Fig. 4-2 The Denver Glass Studio Model beveling machine.

size aluminum oxide wheel for smoothing, both of which are horizontal.

The IB–16, then, has its two horizontal wheels on one side and the vertical array of wheels on the other. The Studio Model has all four of its wheels in the vertical plane facing the worker. There is a single driveshaft for the Studio Model and two for the IB–16, which allows the two speeds this machine offers.

Our feeling is that the Studio Model, both in cost and in what it can do, is a good machine for the average hobbyist. It is true that on a vertical wheel your quality on a straight line suffers somewhat because on it and on the outside curve a little less than half the glass touches the surface of the wheel at one time. Thus the line has a tendency to scallop, whereas on the horizontal wheel almost all of your glass surface touches the wheel, which provides for a much flatter beveled edge all at one time.

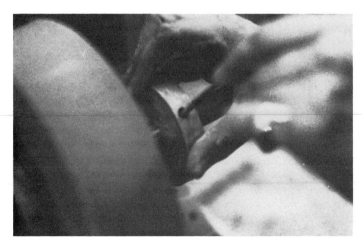

Fig. 4-3 Tightening one of the spacers on the Studio Model beveler.

Fig. 4-4 Shielding the worker from splashing cerium oxide on the Studio Model. The shield is not effective enough to compensate for its getting in your way.

There are ways around this, however, and considering the difference in cost between machines, they are ways worth learning. We will discuss them shortly. There is nothing particularly tricky in learning how to use both vertical and horizontal wheels, and it is both fun and profitable.

Preparing for Roughing: The Horizontal Wheel

The horizontal roughing wheel is cast-iron. This is a function of traditional beveling, when this wheel was made of either cast iron or steel. We prefer cast iron to steel because it is more porous and thus holds the grit on the wheel for a longer time. On a steel wheel the grit will slide off quite rapidly. Care of the cast-iron wheel is minimal. Don't worry about the rust spots that will inevitably develop. The rust comes off once the wheel is put to use. Whatever you do, don't oil this wheel under the mistaken notion that you are helping to preserve it. The grit will immediately slide off the oiled surface, making the wheel useless.

Using a horizontal wheel speeds up beveling time, since you have more surface traveling under the glass edge at one time than with a vertical wheel. Traditionally, beveling machines have a cast iron or steel roughing wheel and a sandstone smoothing wheel. These are both horizontal. The polishing wheels are vertical.

The more horizontal surface you have, the greater is the drag produced on the glass. This is especially true of the smoothing stone. A lot of surface is not essential for polishing, which is why these wheels are vertical, as well as the decreased cost of making them this way. A machine with all horizontal wheels would be much larger than a comparable horizontal/vertical model.

The silicon carbide usually used on the roughing wheel is 80 to 100 grit, although you can use 120 grit. This is almost twice as fine as the 80 and would take longer to do the job, although you would get a smoother roughed bevel. The silicon carbide is poured onto the metal chute over the wheel and water is run into

Fig. 4-5 The cast-iron plate (wheel) and the trough above it. The roughing station is where the beveling process begins.

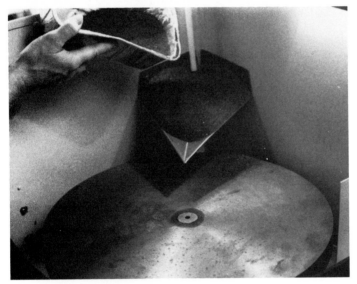

Fig. 4-6 Loading the trough with grit for roughing.

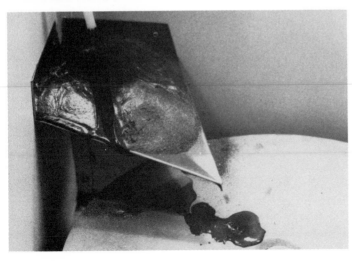

Fig. 4-7 Running water onto the grit to get the proper consistency for good roughing.

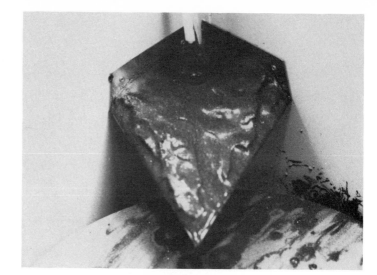

Fig. 4-8 The slurry is formed.

Fig. 4-9 Giving the slurry mix a helping hand.

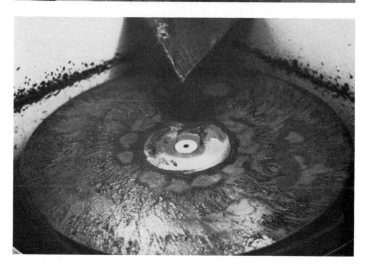

Fig. 4-10 As the slurry goes onto the spinning cast-iron wheel, it is thrown over the surface by centripetal force.

Fig. 4-11 As the wheel spins, the slurry furnishes a powerful grinding surface.

Fig. 4-12 Holding a straight edge at the proper angle for roughing. The slurry drips slowly from the trough at upper right.

Fig. 4-13 Some of the grit will collect against the glass edge, but this is not a problem.

it. The water takes a few minutes to soak in. This mixture should be about the consistency of heavy sour cream. The resultant mass is called *slurry*.

As you run water into the slurry, it will start to drip onto the cast-iron wheel. With the machine turned on, you can control the drip of slurry onto the wheel by increasing or decreasing the water flow. You should allow the wheel to become thoroughly covered with slurry; then turn the water down because the slurry, once properly wetted, will drip down on its own onto the wheel in a sort of gravity-feed process.

You can, and should, reuse the slurry until it is almost white. At this point it is more glass than grit and you can throw it away. About once every four months, with constant use, clean the pan and throw away the used slurry. When scraping anything out of a pan that is galvanized, as the IB–16 pan is, don't use anything that is metal. Once you scratch away the galvanization, the pan will start to rust at the scratch line. Use a wood, plastic, or Teflon scraper to preserve the galvanization.

To rough the glass, hold the edge against the turning wheel in whatever position is most comfortable. There is no right or wrong position. If you can perfect a technique whereby you simply drop a piece of glass onto the wheel and it comes up perfectly beveled, then that is the best way for you.

Before you rough the glass, see if there are any sharp edges on it. These should be smoothed down on the wheel. The same is true if the glass blank doesn't quite fit the pattern. You can bring it precisely to size on the wheel. The cast-iron wheel is an elegant grozzer, and we have used it not only for beveling, but to smooth down the ends of broken bottles or glasses that we want to use in other projects and experiments. Keep experimenting with the

Fig. 4-14 The glass blank for the feather project directly after cutting it from the glass. Note the rough surfaces.

Fig. 4-15 The rough cut of glass with its surfaces seamed smooth on the cast-iron wheel. Note the difference in the edges here and in Fig. 4-14. It takes practically no time to get it to this shape on the machine. Imagine how long it would take to grozze it this smooth by hand.

pressure on the wheel until you discover what amount of pressure brings the fastest results without tiring your arms. This varies to a degree with every worker.

We will begin with $\frac{1}{2}$"-wide bevels because they are the standard art bevels. This is the measurement from the edge of the glass up to the top edge of the angle. A $\frac{1}{2}$" bevel is a convenient size: It is not so wide that the angle becomes too slight to stand out. It is steep enough so that when the beveled piece is leaded in place you can still see an obvious bevel. You don't want the lead came to cover or obscure the beveled edges on which you've worked so hard. We have seen some $\frac{1}{4}$" bevels that all but vanished once the came was applied. Figure that with a $\frac{1}{2}$" bevel you will cover no more than about $\frac{1}{8}$" with the lead came.

As you begin to bevel with either the horizontal or vertical wheel, you will find that in addition to removing some of the glass edge to make an angle you are making that portion of the glass touching the wheel opaque. Having made it opaque, of course you will proceed to make it transparent again with the successive wheels.

The glass becomes opaque—or sandy—because of the abrasive action of the grit. It is similar to the effect from sandblasting. As finer and finer grit is used on the successive wheels, this initial sandiness is ground away. The second wheel, the smoothing stone, gets rid of all this sand. While it will remove the actual pitting—the ground glass surface—it will still leave the new surface cloudy or hazy. While the first wheel shapes the piece fairly rapidly (while opaquing it), the second wheel is most important from an aesthetic viewpoint, since it can aid or abet what you do on the first wheel.

A warning before you begin beveling. While beveling is a lot of fun, and even at the beginning you will come up with all sorts of your own ideas for projects, don't try to learn everything all at once. The danger in overenthusiasm is that you may burn yourself out, start making mistakes, and become discouraged. Many classes in beveling go for about six hours. That's with a lunch break in between. This is plenty of time, so don't try to push beyond that, if that. Even if you are anxious to get the essentials under control, in three days of about six hours' working time, you can become an extremely competent beveler. The rest is practice, which you will be getting as you become involved in all those projects you have already dreamed up.

Straight Lines: Making the Square

Making a square with bevels all around the edges is good practice in straight-line beveling, which may or may not prove to be a simple endeavor for you. It does not necessarily have to be. We start with it because it is basic.

Cut out your square from whatever thickness of plate you have on hand, let's say $\frac{3}{8}''$. This is always a nice size to use for beveling. Don't worry if your cut lines are rough or if the whole square blank looks uneven. We will fix this.

The first thing you will do is to straighten all this out, getting the glass into an even pattern and removing all those grozzing points and prickles. This will not take long on the wheel. Hold the glass flat against it on one edge, then another, until you have the piece satisfactorily shaped. Keep checking it by eye and with a ruler. Once you have it shaped properly, you can begin grinding down the edges to provide your bevels.

Remember to keep a steady drip of water directly into the slurry. You may need to add a little more slurry on the wheel. If so, increase the water drip. The slurry will spread out over the wheel by centripetal force—force throwing it away from the center of this spinning wheel and out toward the rim. It will also, eventually, throw it off the rim. That is one reason why the supply of slurry must be constantly replenished.

You will have to keep stirring the slurry to get the proper mix of water and grit. At first you may have to spend quite a bit of time with this; eventually, you will automatically be able to form the proper consistency. Don't just put a few grams of grit on the trough because it will quickly wash away. Put a whole load of grit on the trough and mix it with the water. The reason why you have a reservoir is because it's inconvenient to keep having to replenish the slurry. Use your hand, not a spatula, to get the feel of the proper mix. The slurry won't bite you, either in the reservoir or on the spinning wheel. You can safely touch the wheel.

Before you put an edge of glass to the wheel, mark BTS (Bevel This Side) on the side to be beveled. It is all too easy, as you turn the glass in your hand, to hold an opposite side to the wheel and come up with a beveled edge you hadn't counted on. It happens all the time.

Never hold the glass so that it fights you, so that you feel awkward with it. There will be an initial awkwardness, true, no matter how you hold the glass to the wheel, but this will quickly pass. If you continue to feel awkward, try holding the glass differently. You should not hold the glass with your index fingers because you will obstruct your view of the edge you are beveling. And if you can't see what you are doing, you will have problems. This is not what we mean by "blind beveling," although it could be classified under that heading.

On the cast-iron roughing wheel it is advantageous to move the glass back and forth across the surface of the wheel. This leads to a more efficient result for a number of reasons.

Moving the Glass Across the Wheel

First, if you try to hold your glass against the wheel without moving it at all, you will quickly find a line appearing in the slurried surface of the cast iron. And soon you will find yourself pressing glass against the bare surface itself. The glass simply wipes away the grit. Moving the glass mixes the surface grit so no bare spots appear from pressure in the one area.

Second, moving the glass increases the beveling speed and thus saves time because you are moving the area to be ground against an already moving surface.

The direction of movement varies with the size of the glass. Small pieces can be moved from side to side or from center to rim, away and toward you. Larger pieces of 4″ or more can be moved from side to side across the wheel, although not in an absolutely straight line across. Even here, too much grit is removed from the wheel surface by the glass. We angle the glass a little,

Fig. 4-16 Roughing a straight edge. The motion is back and forth *across* the wheel.

Fig. 4-17 An uneven edge on a straight-line bevel. Checking as you go helps to keep the procedure straight.

with one edge slightly toward the center, so that the angle of the glass with the wheel rim is maybe 85 degrees. If we move the glass to the left, more glass will be ground off the right edge. If we move the glass to the right, more will be ground off the left edge. This is due to the fact that you are using a spinning wheel with grit particles flowing across it. This paradoxical action of the wheel must be kept in mind when you are attempting to correct uneven bevels.

Whether you hold the glass "against" the wheel rotation or "with" it does not affect the cutting in any way. It may affect your own control of the glass, however. Try it both ways and see which one you are more comfortable with. Some bevelers like to go with or against the wheel depending on the size and/or shape of the piece of glass they are working on.

Don't be afraid to pick up your glass from time to time to see what the bevel looks like. If it is becoming crooked, you can correct it as noted above. The reason for moving the glass in various directions is to achieve the correction factor, which can be confusing to beginners because they tend to forget they are dealing with a grinding wheel, not a continuous belt.

On the vertical roughing wheel, the process is still different so far as motion is concerned. On this wheel the grit is fixed, embedded into the surface of the wheel. Here the glass is moved up and down. Coming down, you remove glass from the top; coming up, you remove glass from the bottom. This is fairly obvious because of the roundness of the wheel and the flatness of the glass.

Once you have roughed one side of your square, go ahead and rough the opposite side. A good technique to use on any four-sided figure, even one that doesn't have parallel edges, is to rough out opposite rather than contiguous sides. What you want to do is to create the same mitre all around. You can do this best in a square or rectangle by holding the glass on end in front of you and checking the bevels for parallel lines. In this way you can readily compare one side with the other. You can't do this if you have roughed two joined edges.

Roughing the Second Edge of the Square

As you continue the roughing procedure, concentrate on maintaining an even flow of motion back and forth across the wheel. Listen for the sound of the wheel on the glass. It will tell you if you need more grit. Try to keep the angle of the glass with the wheel from changing. You may have a tendency to lower the back end of the glass too much as you go along, and this will make the mitre grow. Correct pressure is achieved both by the feel of the glass in your hand and by the sound it makes as it is being ground. It should be a true grinding sound, not a tinkle. Too little pressure against the wheel will round the bevel. You should feel a contact with the wheel all along the side of the glass.

In effect, you will be guided in this procedure by what you feel, hear, and see, as well as by the instinct that you will quickly acquire.

In surveying the edge of the glass as you go along, if you see it begin to go thin and thick, press the bevel more toward the thick end. But keep the same angle up and down or you will end up with two bevels. Remember to stop shy of $\frac{1}{2}''$ on the mitre; try to limit this stop-shy area to $\frac{1}{16}''$.

If you begin to hear a sliding sound rather than a true abrasive sound—one with a sort of jagged rhythm to it—it means that the slurry surface has become very thin beneath the glass. The slurry may have hardened on the trough because you haven't been mixing it with the water. Or you may just be running out. If the slurry "hardens," the water will begin to flow over it rather than through it, and you will be getting more water on the wheel than grit. This sliding sound means that you have too much water on the wheel. Simply remix the slurry on the trough with your hand and reestablish its flow onto the wheel by adjusting the water drip.

After you have done the second side of the square and have matched up the sides for parallel lines, do the next pair of opposite sides and match them up the same way. As you continue moving the glass across the wheel, you may find that you are beginning to sway back and forth. Don't worry about it. The swaying will stop once you have finished roughing.

Once all sides of the square have been roughed, it is time to check the corner angles. Unless all these angles match, you will not have the proper mitres. There are several reasons why this can happen. First, you can cut too steep an angle in one mitre, in which case the angle for that mitre will overreach the corner and intrude into the next mitre's space. Second, you can cut a mitre that slopes too much. You can change the corner angles by changing the angle of the glass against the wheel. Actually, this is "step-beveling," cutting two surfaces in the one bevel.

While there is some room for discrepancy in the corners, there isn't all that much. Of course you are going by eye, not by a micrometer. It won't hurt if the mitre is off the corner of the glass by $\frac{1}{16}''$ or even $\frac{1}{8}''$. The eye won't notice that. But if the mitre is off the corner beyond $\frac{1}{8}''$, the eye will catch it, especially if the piece is to be joined with others in a leaded panel, where all the mitred corners join together in a straight line.

Working with the Beveled Angle

While roughing, you should try to keep the angle of the glass and the wheel the same throughout. If you change this angle gradually, you will make the mitre grow. If you change it abruptly, you may end up with a slight ridge. The beveled angle can also come out rounded or with an irregular belly.

When grinding out these types of defects, you should ease up on your pressure or you may widen the entire mitre beyond the prescribed $\frac{1}{2}''$.

Many problems with mitres and angles can be avoided if you remember to come both ways on the cast-iron wheel. Try to make even swings right and left.

Also remember that most defects can be fixed. Such things as uneven bevels happen all the time. Just go back from the widest part and straighten it all out. Don't give in to the tendency to overcompensate.

In correcting a ridge in the bevel, it is possible to widen the bevel on one side over the other sides. If this happens, first check to see how much you have gone over. Don't be such a perfectionist that you automatically start grinding the other sides to match. If you go over the $\frac{1}{2}''$ margin by $\frac{1}{16}''$ or less, just leave it alone. Probably the eye won't pick it up. If you have gone over by $\frac{1}{8}''$, try to widen the other sides to match. If you go over by $\frac{1}{4}''$, you should probably redo the piece.

Many beginners feel uneasy about the angle they are creating. They tend to put more pressure on the ends of the bevel than in the middle—at least in a fairly large piece of glass (more than 6 inches). Beware of applying uneven pressure. Try to keep the pressure balanced.

The roughing stone can be a difficult one to get used to. If you are having trouble, go ahead and straighten out a poor angle on the smoothing stone—the next step—rather than dwelling on the cast-iron wheel. This procedure has some advantages. The stone removes glass much more slowly than does the cast-iron wheel, so you are unlikely to compound your present problem. There is also the possibility of becoming too desperately involved with this first wheel. If so, the stone will give you a welcome break, and you can come back to the roughing wheel with a fresh outlook.

Fig. 4-18 Placing a ruler behind the glass is an easy way to measure the width of a mitre.

At least one teacher we know, Linda Neely, prefers to start students on the smoothing stone if they are having trouble roughing. She does the initial roughing for them and then has them take the piece to the stone to acquire confidence. After that they learn the roughing wheel.

Working on your own, you will go first to the roughing wheel. But that doesn't mean you are stuck to it until you get it perfect. Don't go around in circles with it. Take the rough with the smooth.

Rough Hints

1. Beware of a silicon carbide buildup on the cast-iron wheel. This can actually mark the glass with a line down the surface of the bevel. Ridges of grit on the wheel can occur if there is not enough water. The proper mix is essential and should be constantly checked.

2. Just because you have the mitred angles fixed in place when you are finished with the cast-iron wheel, it doesn't mean that they can't be moved on the smoothing stone. This can be frustrating, but keep it in mind; you may not want to spend time getting angles absolutely perfect on the roughing wheel, only to mar them in the following procedure. We get them set on the roughing wheel but depend on the smoothing stone for a final permanence. The smoothing stone is the last stone in the process that can actually move these mitred corners. The polishing wheels can soften these angles but not move them.

3. When we talk of moving angles or correcting any defect, we are also talking about removing glass. If you have to remove so much glass to correct a defect that you distort the area, the correction wasn't worth it.

4. When you are finished working on the cast-iron stone, wash

Fig. 4-19 The star accidentally roughed on one wrong surface. This is a nice effect, but only if you planned it that way.

the glass and your hands thoroughly. Otherwise you will inevitably carry silicon carbide to the next wheel. That's how you end up scratching glass. Ideally you should use a different apron for each station, although we don't know anyone who does.

5. When you straighten an angle, do it gradually or you will end up with two bevels. If that should happen, put the piece back to the wheel and let the wheel surface be a guide. While the angle is riding, press in the one spot to get the proper $\frac{1}{2}''$, and then carry that angle along the length of the bevel.

6. If you bevel on the wrong side, you have two ways out. One is to convince everyone that you did it purposely. But then you can't act surprised if you have one bevel staring at you and another staring at the wheel. It also helps if you have selected a thick piece of plate: $\frac{1}{4}''$ won't do, unless you have a mere "skin" bevel on one side and a steeper one on the other. If you have been beveling a $\frac{3}{8}''$, however, you can get a nice effect with bevels on both sides. But, of course, you now have to go ahead and make all the other bevels to match. The second way out is to scrap the piece, and next time remember to mark the surface you want to bevel.

7. All wet bevels, roughed or smoothed or polished, look terrific. If you can figure out a way to keep your bevels from drying, you can cut your working time by 75 percent. When bevels dry, defects start to appear.

8. If you are right-handed, you will probably automatically do your work on the left-hand side of the glass, holding it with the left hand while guiding and manipulating it with the right. If you are left-handed, the positions are just the reverse. In any case, work in whatever position is most comfortable. Don't get in your own way.

9. Especially when using the roughing wheel, take off rings and watches, or you may bevel angles on them as well as the glass.

10. You can bevel a fairly large piece of plate on the IB–16 (or comparable machine) by removing the rubber margin that surrounds the roughing wheel on three sides. Just come across a corner of the cast-iron wheel down toward the floor. You can do long pieces of glass in this way, although it is fairly awkward.

Outside Curves: Making the Shield

The shield project is designed to teach outside curves, but there is no reason why you also can't make a lovely piece of beveled glass to use for decoration. When you are finished, you can bore a hole in it and hang it in a window for effect. If you want to, you can use a piece of glue-chip plate or some old textured plate glass, which can be found in junkyards. The surface modifications in these types of glass add to the fun of creating while you learn the basic techniques.

Cutting the Shield

The shield is rather simple, with a straight edge above and two outside curves flaring from either end of the straight edge to the bottom point. You could also make a shield that has a top inside curve instead of the straight edge, since inside curves will be discussed next. It would probably be a good idea to make both.

Cutting the shield pattern from plate glass is not difficult. You can score it and grozze out the score lines with heavy-duty grozzing pliers, or you can break out these gradual curves with running pliers.

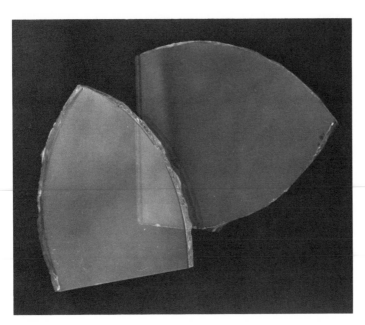

Fig. 4-20 One piece of the shield pattern broken out of the glass blank and ready for the roughing station.

Another way to break out the sides easily is to double score them, making a score on the top and back sides of the plate. That is easy to do with this simple pattern. Double scoring can be broken out with regular rather than heavy-duty running pliers. It also makes it easier to break out the glass with regular grozzing pliers.

If you are using running pliers, it might be helpful to run the score from top to bottom—that is, from the straight edge to the point—since you may have more excess glass at the "top" than at the "bottom." Also, the curve becomes more acute toward the point, and your break line may not follow your score line in this area. But you will probably have to grozze at the point in any event. Just rough-grozze where absolutely necessary with pliers and leave the fine grozzing to the machine.

The Technique of the Glass Against the Wheel

As usual, the first thing to do is to even up the glass blank to match the pattern and grozze the rough edges down. After you have done this, you are ready to rough the sides. Our pattern shows three sides: two outside curves and a straight edge (see Fig. 4-20). Do the straight edge last.

The technique for roughing outside curves is different from that of roughing straight lines. In this case, you will not be traveling back and forth across the wheel to any extent, although you may want to move the glass slightly. Instead of going back and forth, you will be imparting an arcing motion to the glass. This, plus the shape of the piece, may make it more difficult to get comfortable with the glass in your hand than with the square.

Beginners tend to make their outside curves too slight along the mitres, or, in other words, too thick on the edge. We find that there are several ways to rough this curve, depending on the size of the glass.

With fairly large pieces of glass, where it will obviously be extremely awkward to do the entire curve at one time, do small sections at a time, holding the glass at a fairly steep angle. Try not to cover more surface edge than you can handle, imparting this arcing or rolling motion to feed the next section onto the wheel. You can control the glass more effectively this way than by holding it still; the motion also helps to prevent facets from forming between the areas being worked on.

The other way is to arc the entire curve at one time, forming it as a complete section. Here the glass must be small enough to be able to control it. Both ways will work well once you get used to them.

We hold the glass at slightly less than a right angle to the surface of the wheel. If we are doing a long edge, we have to be careful that the portion of it toward the rim doesn't grind faster than that toward the center of the wheel, where there is less grinding surface. This tendency can be offset by increasing the pressure you exert or the amount of time you spend on that particular side.

Another way to control this—and the way that we prefer—is to turn the piece around by using the reverse half of the wheel. If you have been using the right half, with the straight edge facing toward the center turn to the left half. The straight edge will now be facing the rim. Attempting to turn the piece in your hands without making this transfer leaves you with no way to hold it effectively or comfortably, since the beveled edge is now facing you directly.

The outside curve of course is part of a circle. One of the most difficult aspects of an outside curve is maintaining the angle. Be careful that you are not just roughing the glass at the edge.

Maintaining the Angle

As you work the outside curve across the wheel, try to hold the same angle all around. It is better to start out with a $\frac{1}{2}''$ angle rather than timidly going for a $\frac{1}{4}''$ one and assuming you can always make it wider. It is more difficult to widen the angle than to get it right immediately. If necessary, mark the width of the angle with a ruler and a marking pencil and use the line as a guide. If you keep the edge steady and check it from time to time, you will be able to keep the mitre in line.

With an outside curve, as with a circle, you work from glass edge to beveled edge. You can't match up sides, as with a square, because there are no sides to match up. At least with the outside curve, there are certain relationships: for instance, the two mitred angles at the top and the one at the point.

The angle at the point tends to throw many students. Don't even think about it as you start to rough. If you watch your arcing motion, watch your width, and keep an eye on the thickness of the edge, the mitred angle will come right where it should be—directly in line with the point of the glass. Only when you try too hard will you find yourself in trouble. Relax. Beveling is supposed to be fun. Don't trap yourself at this point. If the angle goes crooked here, it might be best to leave it alone and pick it up again on the smoothing stone. If you try to straighten it up, pushing it back and forth and trying to align it with the glass, you will just be removing more and more glass until you have nothing left. The roughing wheel takes glass away much faster than you may realize.

Mitreing the Curve

Outside curves are the most difficult shapes to mitre. We start them by selecting one side and beveling it all at one shot. We rough the entire edge with a smooth rolling motion, holding the glass diagonally across the outer margin of the wheel. This motion is repeated two or three times. Looking at the bevel shows us that it is getting slightly wider toward the point, which is that portion closer to the rim of the wheel. We twist slightly to the left, opposite to the way we are standing, and replace the glass on the wheel. Now the point is facing the center of the wheel. In a short time the mitre has evened off. This process is repeated until the width of the mitre has been reached. We have not paid attention to the lower angle at the point, but, because we have made sure all our other measurements are accurate, this one also has to be.

Next, we rough the opposing outside curve. We do it precisely the same way, paying no attention to that bottom mitre. Again, everything falls into place. Checking the bottom angle shows us that the mitre is fairly well positioned, although not perfect. We have allowed enough thickness of the angle here so that glass can be removed from either side without diminishing the area, even if the angle has to be moved quite a bit from one side or the other.

One thing we do as we come down to this bottom angle is to be careful not to intrude upon it. We come up *to* it, not upon it. Therefore, we can leave a slight buffer zone to either side of it, which comes in handy for setting it right on the proper spot when we get to it. The last step is to finish the mitred angles on the smoothing stone.

With the outside curve, as you work each section, you can't spend too much time on one area or you will end up with facets. You must work so that each section contacts the next smoothly, so that the basic shape is maintained. When you take it off the cast-iron plate, you may find a slightly rounded mitre to the curve. This should be flattened on the smoothing stone.

Mitre applies to the width of the bevel, not the length. The reason the bevel is rounded when it comes off the cast-iron plate is that the abrasive on the wheel doesn't allow it to contact the surface in a flat manner. But this is made up on the smoothing stone, where the glass contacts the surface directly with just water between wheel and glass. The rounded mitre flattens right out.

Outside Curves: Making the Circle

When you work with a circle, try to relate glass edge to beveled edge, since there are no sides. There is no way that you can do a circular bevel in one fell swoop. You must do it a section at a time, roughing it out slowly and trying not to allow flat spots, or facets, to intrude between these work areas. The rhythm is important in beveling a circle. It is important to know when to leave an area and move on to the next. It is also important that you have a fairly large piece of glass to bevel; the smaller the glass, the more difficult it is to hold against the wheel. A reasonable beveled circle might be 4″ in diameter. Circles get smaller more rapidly than you might think as you try constantly to even up the bevel. Pretty soon you are beveling your fingers.

Cutting the Circle

Quickest results, and probably the best, are obtained with a circle cutter. There are numbers of these on the market that will cut circles of many different diameters. When cutting circles from plate, we recommend that you double score—that is, score on both sides. (See our book *Crafting in Glass*.) This makes it easier to "press out" the score line, and it gives you as a result a very neat margin around the circle. As with other shapes, you may get a circle that requires a certain amount of grozzing. Let the cast-iron wheel take care of this.

If you cut your circle freehand from a pattern, you can also double score here. Some people do not want to take the time to double score, or they feel they will make the obverse score slightly inaccurate to the first and ruin the glass. Double scoring is a good way to go, but you can score a circle of plate on one side and break it out either with grozzing pliers or with running pliers with the usual technique. The only problem is that it's more difficult with plate than with the usual $\frac{1}{8}''$ stained glass. However, it is up to you. No matter how you get your circle, once it is ready, you can take it directly to the cast-iron wheel.

Sectional Roughing

Every beginner should include a circle as a beveling procedure right at the start. We have found that no other shape gave us so much technique for the amount of time spent. In addition, the circle is an intriguing figure.

As we said earlier, when you bevel a circle, there are no sides to match up. You can only relate glass edge and beveled angle. Your hand must learn how to carry that mitre around the entire periphery of the glass edge. You have to stay in one place long enough to give the wheel a chance to provide the proper angle; then you are off to carry that angle around to the next area. The whole trick of outside curves is getting your hand to learn the changing of the turn so that the mitre continues smoothly and no facets form between stopping points. Once you start the turn, the angle is liable to change—either to flatten or steepen—and if you allow it to do this, you are in trouble. Once you have permitted one section of the circle to hold a bevel that is different from the rest, you must enforce the one on the other. This can be extremely frustrating, but you will learn a great deal about beveling technique.

Away-from-the-Wheel Versus Against-the-Wheel Beveling

As you stand facing the cast-iron wheel, you will notice that it (probably) turns clockwise. This means that you can use it in two ways: You can hold your glass to the right-hand side of the wheel, in which case the wheel's surface will be passing toward you, pushing at the glass; or you can hold the glass to the left-hand side of the wheel, in which case the pull will be away from you.

Some workers prefer one side of the wheel; others prefer the other side. So far as the grinding effect is concerned, there is really little difference. There is a difference in the degree of comfort in holding the glass. You may be able to achieve more pressure of glass to wheel with the force of the wheel driving *at* you rather than away from you. This is particularly true when grinding circles and outside curves. On the other hand, you may find that you can guide the glass best with the wheel spinning away from you. There appears to be a difference in choice only when small pieces are being ground—or at least pieces that do not take up the major surface of the wheel. Large pieces of glass can be done on both the right-hand and left-hand sides of the wheel. However, since circles involve sectional beveling no matter how large they are, you always have a choice of going with the wheel or against the wheel here. At least try both ways, if only to feel the difference to your hand. You might prefer one over the other, or you may find that it makes little difference. Some workers use against-the-wheel grinding to get a lot of glass ground away quickly; they use away-from-the-wheel grinding to achieve finishing touches. In many instances, that's the way we prefer it.

Small-Piece Grinding

When you have a number of small pieces of glass to bevel, the roughing process can become rather painful. It is here that we advise the use of rubber fingertips. Although you can put your finger against the grinding wheel with no ill effect, constant slipping of your finger against it, with the pressure of grinding behind it, will lead to beveled flesh and the use of many bandaids. Once you get some of these finger nicks, and once the grit from the wheel gets into them, you will have sore reminders of what is supposed to be your fun hobby. There are several ways out of this. The easiest is probably to acquire rubber fingertips. Easier than this, at least initially, is to avoid grinding pieces that are too small to hold easily. If you insist that small pieces are necessary to your artistic expression, then be prepared to have your fingers pay the price.

In some cases, you could make a holder for the small pieces of glass so that you can do them and still not look and feel as though you'd put your fingers in a pencil sharpener. Such a holder can be devised using jeweler's wax on a piece of wood, with the glass to be beveled stuck firmly into it. Unfortunately, you are actually "blind beveling" here, since the wood prevents you from seeing the angle. We have tried this method, and it works fairly well. You have to be careful that the jeweler's wax doesn't become cold and thus brittle. The glass pieces won't stick if it does, and they will be swept away by the force of the wheel and undoubtedly break. Although the holder may seem awkward at first, you will get used to it fairly quickly. Needless to say, a holder isn't necessary on large pieces. Your own two hands are best here.

Inside Curves: Using the Edge

It is perfectly possible to do inside curves on the cast-iron wheel, although it is much simpler to do them on the vertical wheel. This technique is limited, however, because you must use the edge of the wheel and work in a downward direction from it. On the horizontal wheel, you are limited as to size, since the boxing of the machine doesn't allow for oversized pieces. On a single-station cast-iron wheel, you can do inside curves on very large pieces— although it is hardly worthwhile to acquire such a device for this purpose alone.

On standard machines, you will use the outside edge of the wheel, anywhere from $\frac{1}{4}''$ to $\frac{1}{8}''$, depending on how tight your curve is. We find it best to work against the spin of the wheel here. You can hold the glass firmly and guide the curve slowly along the entire edge. Use some extra water on the slurry to make sure that plenty of abrasive gets out to the edge of the wheel.

Since the cast-iron plate is perfectly flat, you don't have to worry about any pitch of the wheel throwing off your curve. Practice cutting out and roughing some inside curves at random. Once you have become proficient at the technique, you should try to make an actual shape. We will make a star, a shape with plenty of inside curves, using the vertical wheel (although there is nothing to prevent you from doing one on the cast-iron edge as well).

It is a good idea to make star-shaped pieces asymmetric. This is good practice for teaching yourself a different inside curve on all four sides, rather than doing the same inside curve, over and over again.

Preparing for Roughing: The Vertical Wheel

The vertical roughing wheel employs a diamond surface. It would be impossible to employ a cast-iron wheel and grit combination in this position because the grit would simply fly off.

Diamond wheels come in a number of different sizes. They are fairly expensive, so you should choose the size that will be the most flexible for the work you will be doing. We find that an 8″ wheel answers most of our occasions, although you could also get a 6″ and a 4″ wheel. Problems can arise if the wheel is too large for the radius of your inside curve. In this case, you may have to go to a smaller size wheel and keep changing wheels to match up with the design. This not only can be time-consuming, but it can be expensive. It would be best to design your pieces

Fig. 4-21 A vertical diamond wheel on the IB–16. The water jet shows the normal amount of water applied.

Fig. 4-22 Attaching the diamond wheel to the right-hand bay of the Denver Studio Model. This machine has one locking flange and one regular flange on the inside wheel, so you can move this wheel or the outside one into the hub. All the nuts are self-tightening. After you hand-tighten them, they will tighten further as the machine is operated. You may need a wrench to loosen them.

for the wheel that you have. You can get some tight curves from the 8″ wheel if you just have patience. It is simply a matter of carefully grinding one surface of the curve and then the other.

Another way to get these curves is with a cone wheel. These wheels are available, but they do not apply to the IB–16. One nice machine that uses the cone wheel is the Somaca Glass Lathe. It can be used for engraving as well as other fascinating things. However, the last thing you need at this point is another type wheel, and we don't recommend acquiring one just to do inside curves. Stick to the diamond wheel for the time being.

Inside Curves: Making the Star

The first thing you want to do with your diamond wheel is to turn the water onto it. You must keep the diamond wheel wet; running it dry against the glass will ruin the wheel. Keep a wet sponge below it touching the surface of the wheel. This is not to keep the wheel wet (the water jet will do that), but to keep the water from splashing you.

Cut out the rough glass blank of the star pattern, then remove all the rough edges and shape the piece. The diamond wheel we recommend is 100 grit, so if you are used to using 100-grit silicon carbide on the cast-iron wheel, you will get the same effect with the diamond. Actually, you will probably find that the diamond wheel is quicker and cleaner than the cast-iron one. It is of course rotating more swiftly than the horizontal wheel because it is smaller. Other than that, it does cut better. You will find that you have to use a firmer pressure with the diamond wheel than with the cast-iron wheel.

The beginning angle of the inside curve is the same with both the cast-iron and diamond wheel. To begin, put the lower edge of the glass down on the wheel and hold it to start the grinding

Fig. 4-23 *Left:* the star pattern and the glass rough. *Top right:* the glass rough for an S shape. *Below right:* the oaktag pattern and below that the finished bevel.

process. Don't let your fingers hide the area where you will be working. Hold the curve vertically to the vertical wheel—not, as some people think, horizontally across it. If you try to grind this way, holding the glass across with the wheel spinning straight up and down, you will scallop the glass.

What you want to do is hold the edge of the curve parallel to the rim surface of the wheel. By doing this, you can make outside curves as well on this wheel. Once you have the edges parallel, keep turning the glass so that each section touching the wheel remains parallel to its rim. Turn just enough to keep the working edge parallel to the edge of the wheel and stop the turn when it looks like you are going too far. The object is to keep the edge

Fig. 4-24 The top edge shows the two arcs that you can get on the glass surface with the diamond wheel, by either under- or over-turning the glass against the wheel. The working area should always be parallel to the rim of the wheel. The bottom edge shows the proper bevel you get by doing this when working with an inside curve.

Fig. 4-25 Seaming the edge of a glass blank on the vertical diamond prior to forming the rough bevel. This makes the edge smooth, removing all sharp pinpoints that may remain from cutting and breaking.

that you are cutting directly parallel to the wheel's edge. Never go with the shape of the wheel—that is, up and down, tipping and rolling the glass to conform with the round surface. Once you start this kind of movement to conform to the shape of the wheel, you will scallop the glass at the pivot point.

If you are getting some scalloping in the bevel area, it means that you are applying uneven pressure as you turn the glass. Probably you are trying too hard. Just relax and be prepared to ruin a number of pieces of glass before you get the touch.

Even before you touch the glass to the wheel, you will see another considerable difference between this wheel and the cast-

Fig. 4-26 Straight edges can also be seamed on the vertical diamond wheel.

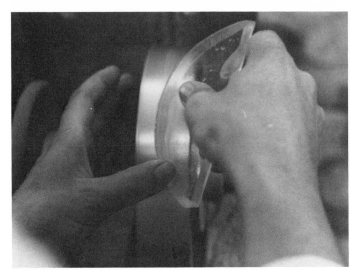

Fig. 4-27 Roughing on the vertical diamond. The roughing process begins at the lowest portion of the glass and progresses toward the top. Here we show a single upward sweep to demonstrate the position of the glass against the wheel. The part being ground is always parallel to the outer rim of the wheel. The glass therefore must be turned as you continue to rough.

iron one. The diamond wheel splashes water at you. Wear an apron, and expect to get wet. This of course adds to the excitement of making your first bevel with a diamond wheel. But it all takes getting used to.

Rough Hints

1. Wear old clothes and a plastic apron to avoid getting wet.
2. Practice the difference in touch between the diamond wheel and the cast-iron one.
3. Keep the working surface of the glass parallel to the rim of the wheel. This means you must turn it in the horizontal plane.

Fig. 4-28 Roughing an outside curve on the vertical diamond wheel. The part of the mitre being ground is parallel to the outer rim of the wheel. Continue up the mitre toward the point of the glass.

Fig. 4-29 As you come to the point of the glass, turn the glass so that the next section of the mitre is parallel to the outer rim of the wheel. Note the different position of the glass compared to its position in Figs. 4-27 and 4-28.

4. Work the glass edge with just the right pressure on the surface of the wheel keeping the glass rotating slowly to avoid flat spots.

5. Don't tip and roll the glass to conform to the shape of the wheel. If you do this, you will have a straight bevel going across the curve instead of one that will be the same radius as the curve. You will also have an uneven surface thickness.

6. If you are right-handed, start at the left side of the glass. Starting in the middle of the glass may help you find your angle better. Slowly come up and down. Be careful you don't dip the fore edge of the glass into the wheel. Keep your glass on a perfectly flat plane while turning it.

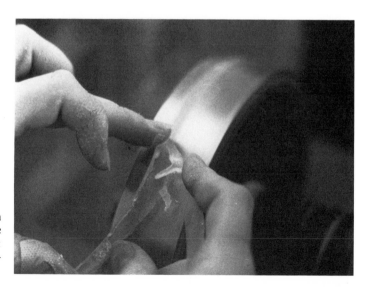

Fig. 4-30 Completing one turn on the vertical diamond for the inside curve. Note the position of the glass: The edge being ground is still parallel to the outer rim of the wheel.

Fig. 4-31 The margins of this inside curve are even . . .

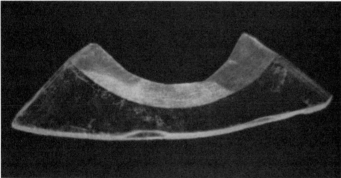

Fig. 4-32 . . . but poorly roughed.

Fig. 4-33 An inside curve held flat against the diamond wheel. The roughing is uneven because more grinding is done at the points of the shape than at the curve. This is why you must move the glass in the horizontal plane so that the edge is parallel to the rim of the wheel.

Fig. 4-34 Checking the rough on an S shape.

7. Try not to let your glass slip off the edge of the wheel, as this will ridge the surface of the bevel.

8. The diameter of the wheel you use will determine the amount of glass surface that will be touching the surface of the wheel. On an 8″ wheel you will have $\frac{1}{2}$″ to $\frac{3}{4}$″ of the flat surface of the glass touching. On a smaller wheel, say 4″, you will have less than one half of that amount of glass touching.

9. Overturning the glass, that is, turning it too acutely in the horizontal plane, will leave the ends mostly untouched. Turning the glass too slightly, on the other hand, will leave the center thicker than the two ends.

Working with the Angle

Think of the inside curve as being divided into two surfaces—a right and a left. These opposite sides must have precisely the same angle of bevel if the piece is to look right. Most beginners working with inside curves tend to make the angle too steep. This is opposite to outside curves, where they tend to make the angle too slight.

Before going too far, perhaps after three or four trips over the wheel, stop, wash the piece to remove debris, and look to see (1) if the angle is getting too steep, and (2) if the angles of the right and left sides match. If the angle is too steep, shave it so that it will come out more in width than in steepness. If the angles of the two sides don't match, correct this now. After you have ground away a considerable quantity of glass, this defect may not be so easily correctable, if at all. Remember that the edge continues to thin out. If it becomes too thin, it will start to crumble and throw your whole bevel awry.

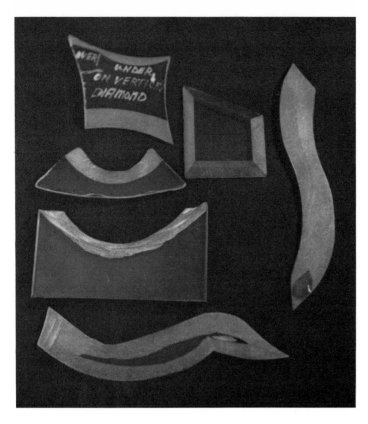

Fig. 4-35 Diamonds in the rough—
or some roughs from the diamond
wheel. The second piece from the
bottom is an example of what happens when the wheel gets out of
control—either from too much
pressure, from running too close to
the edge, or from not checking as
you go. The gouging of this surface
plus the uneven bevel margin are
hard to repair.

If you have a small, tight curve to bevel, you can still do this
on a fairly large wheel such as the 8″. You would probably get a
better inside curve if you used a smaller wheel, but it isn't necessary
to spend the additional money for another wheel.

Maintaining Even Pressure

Pressure is perhaps even more critical on the diamond wheel
than on the cast-iron stone. For one thing, the diamond turns
much more rapidly than the stone and the pressure is thereby
magnified. The pressure should not be too soft or too hard. Listen
for the sound that each wheel makes until you can recognize the
difference immediately. Too soft a pressure over a long period of
time will ruin a diamond wheel. It will also produce a rounded
surface on the glass, which you then must work to get out. The
edge of the glass, as usual, is your best guide. Stop frequently
and look at the edge. Check the width of the edge along one leg
of the curve against that of the other. You can go mostly by eye;
you don't have to measure.

Applying too much pressure can cause you to lose control of
the piece and scallop the bevel. Don't be in a hurry to get the
angle placed as quickly as possible. There is something about

Fig. 4-36 Beveled outer and inner curves. *Top left:* a finished shield that was inadvertently scratched—and ruined—somewhere along the line. Note how the scratch becomes the focus of attention. *Bottom left:* the upper surface was beveled on the wrong side. *Right:* a shallow bevel. This mitre is acceptable if you want this kind of effect. But much of it could be lost when you lead the piece. It could work as a free-hanging object.

using the diamond wheel that makes one feel powerful and sometimes too bossy over the glass. When this happens, it is time to step back from this overconfidence. If you don't, you will probably ruin the piece by grinding out of control. Remember, you are supposed to be doing the guiding, not the wheel.

Other Shapes

In addition to doing inside curves on the diamond wheel, you can do straight lines or outside curves just as well as on the cast-iron wheel. There is some difference, however. With straight lines you would, as before, do the opposite sides first so as to match them up, then the two sides in between. The angles between the mitres will fall into place if you match the sides up properly as to width and the proper slant.

On the cast-iron wheel it doesn't matter if you overshoot the angles a bit, but on the diamond it does matter. Here you must go very carefully from bevel to bevel, rather than from glass edge to edge. Otherwise you will wear the bevels down. The difference is that the diamond wheel removes glass very quickly, much more so than the cast-iron wheel. You can remove so much glass so rapidly with the diamond that there is literally no margin for error on the mitred angles. This is why we suggest the stone wheel for correcting small errors. It is best to remove glass from critical areas on the vertical stone rather than trying to get them perfectly set with the diamond. It takes somewhat longer to do this—you have to learn how much excess to leave at the angles—but you'll throw away fewer bevels.

Of course, you can stay with the horizontal cast-iron wheel if

Fig. 4-37 A small decorative halo and a beveled circle. These were pieces of scrap glass that we recycled into practice pieces. This circle must go back to the smoothing stone to remove the facets.

you have one for straights. The IB–16 has both wheels; the Studio Model has only vertical wheels. The more wheels you have the more options you can consider. Most hobbyists will use a small vertical machine and thus will be working mainly with the diamond wheel. Because it is all too easy to overshoot the corner angles with this wheel, you will have to practice to get them right. Nevertheless, we prefer the diamond wheel to the cast-iron one.

One question usually arises: Why a vertical diamond rather than a horizontal one? For one thing, a horizontal diamond would be too expensive considering the amount of surface to be covered. Also, it is more expensive to furnish horizontal than vertical wheels in general. As a space saver, you can't beat vertical wheels. Since most of the cost of the beveling machine is tied up in the wheels, the smaller they are, the cheaper the machine.

To reiterate, you can do any shape on vertical wheels so long as you remember to take care with those corner mitres.

It is possible to do a tight inside curve on a diamond wheel that is actually too large to accommodate it readily. As a final practice project on the diamond wheel, you might want to go through these specific steps.

Let's postulate a tight inside curve for which you would ordinarily use a 4″ diamond wheel. It is far too tight to do on an 8″ wheel, but you don't have a 4″ wheel, and you don't want to

Project: A Tight Inside Curve on a Large Wheel

invest in another diamond. When you try to do this tight curve on the 8″ wheel, however, the tightness will not allow the glass to contact in the center.

The trick is to start on the end, slowly removing glass and lowering the plane at that point. Next, slowly start removing glass toward the middle, just to make enough room as you approach the center so that you can get around to the other end. Turn the glass very slowly. You may still have some extra thickness in the center; use the wheel to bring this down.

Never use the edge of the diamond. The edge will only ridge the glass. Once you make the original rough shape with the diamond, you will have no trouble smoothing or polishing it on wheels of the same diameter. It will sit directly flush with the wheel now that it is ground.

So, go to it.

CHAPTER 5

The Second Station: Smoothing

Each step in the beveling process leads you closer to the completed, sparkling piece of glass that you are entitled to think of as your own creation. When measured against this ideal, the glass in its present rough state may seem to be far from what you had in mind. But don't worry. As grizzled as it may look at present, it will shortly be transformed into the airy bit of reflective material that you began with. It's a Cinderella process, and the beveling machine is the fairy godmother.

Like most fairy godmothers, the beveling machine uses a magic wand. In this case, it is the smoothing stone, which is the heart of the beveling process. It is the point where the ground glass starts to become a bevel, and it is also the point where it can become a poor or a superlative one. Every step beyond this only adds luster to what the smoothing stone has accomplished. Luster in itself is neither good nor bad. The polishing wheels will shine up facets as well as smooth surfaces. It is up to you to know the difference and to admit to whatever flaws you have put into the bevel at this second stage of the process—as well as feeling proud of those you have removed. Unfortunately, the ones you have removed don't show.

The aluminum oxide stone wheel must have water running on it at all times while it is in use. The wheel is the abrasive, the water is the coolant.

A new aluminum oxide stone wheel, as is also the case with natural sandstone, will at first absorb water into the wheel directly under the spigot. The water will not at first flow out over the surface. After a short time, however, the stone will begin to hold water on the surface, allowing for spark-free smoothing.

Use your supply of paper towels to wipe the glass so that you can see how the smoothing is progressing. To see what you have accomplished, you must actually pick up the glass, dry it, and look

The Aluminum Oxide Stone

91

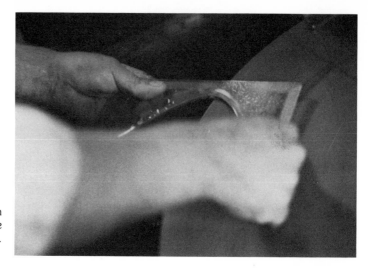

Fig. 5-1 Smoothing a $\frac{1}{2}''$ bevel on the horizontal smoothing stone, the straight margin of an inside curve. (Courtesy The Glass Bevel.)

at it with direct, natural and reflected light. Here you will see if you have an uneven surface from the cast-iron wheel. You may see facets or waves and sand in the bevel.

Sand on the surface of the bevel looks like the effects of sand-blasting. If you don't get rid of all the sand at this stage—even to the last grain—it will show up forcibly when you polish the bevel.

As we have mentioned, the cast-iron wheel is perfectly flat. However, this is not true of the smoothing stone. When the manufacturer dresses the wheel, he puts a 4-degree pitch on it. The purpose of the pitch is to cut down the amount of drag this stone produces. If the wheel were perfectly flat, the entire bevel would rest on the surface at one time. This would make the drag so great that it would be all but impossible to hold on to the glass. Also, this pitch allows you to get your fingers under the glass; this wouldn't be possible if the stone were flat.

But, you may say, the cast-iron wheel is perfectly flat and the drag is not insuperable. True, but on the cast-iron wheel you have the grit between the bevel and the wheel surface, which breaks the drag. On the smoothing stone you are grinding directly onto the stone's surface. That makes for a lot of suction.

The aluminum oxide stone is really not a stone at all: It is a man-made wheel. However, the terms *stone* and *wheel* are used interchangeably, so there is more confusion than clarity in trying to separate them. We will refer to it both ways. The aluminum oxide wheel (or stone) can be cast from a mold with a pitch already imposed. If not, the pitch is put on with a special machine.

Natural sandstone, the first material used for smoothing, is flat and must be dressed, since this is actual stone, not molded material.

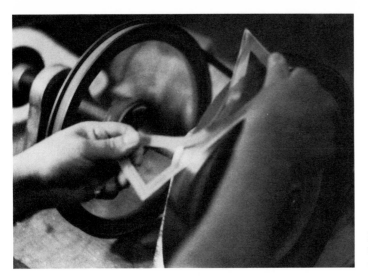

Fig. 5-2 Smoothing on the vertical wheel, a $\frac{1}{2}''$ bevel on an inside curve. (Courtesy The Glass Bevel.)

What is the best material for smoothing glass? Some bevelers absolutely insist on using only natural sandstone, which comes from Newcastle, England. Their claim is that the end result shows the difference. But sandstone, a very rough stone, has its difficulties. Many impurities are already embedded within it, and many are not particularly amiable to glass or to the beveling process. Some of these are iron deposits and granite. Granite, especially, will scratch your glass, and this is a frustrating experience. When dressing the stone, you must try to get below these areas. If there is a great deal of granite or iron showing on the surface at the time the pitch is put on, the manufacturer removes as much of the stone as possible in attempting to get rid of these noxious elements. That is why these stones are sold in varying thicknesses.

Initially, sandstone was pink in color. But it seems the more that is mined, the more the color changes to brown, which is probably the result of impurities. Sometimes the manufacturer cannot remove any more harmful impurities from the stone without sacrificing the entire stone. In this case, he may take an ice pick and chip out the worst ones. Then, with a blowtorch, he melts paraffin into the resulting holes. These paraffin patches wear with the wheel surface. Of course this leaves some areas where no grinding occurs, but this doesn't matter, since the wheel, in turning, offers plenty of surface.

So, natural stone has its problems. Probably these are the very reasons why some workers prefer it; it's a challenge. We are happy working with the artificial but comparatively problem-free aluminum oxide stone.

The aluminum oxide produces a dense, hard stone. It takes a long time to dress—that is, give it the proper shape and pitch for

Natural Versus Man-Made Stone

beveling. It is not something you will want to try to do by hand. Let an expert with the proper machinery do the job. There is a cost factor of about $100 to dress a sandstone. This may or may not be figured in with the cost of the stone. The aluminum oxide stone is already dressed when you purchase it. It need not be dressed further unless you want a special shape.

Wear factors are about the same for each type of smoothing stone, provided the density of each is about the same.

Many people seem to think that something man-made cannot be quite as good as something natural. This reasoning itself seems natural. But we find it, at least so far as the aluminum oxide stone is concerned, *not* the case.

The Smoothing Stone Technique

On the smoothing stone there is no traveling back and forth across the surface as with the cast-iron station. You will see, as you place your bevel against the stone, that a bubble appears at the point of contact. This bubble indicates where the cutting or wearing surface is located. It is in this spot that glass is being removed. The technique of smoothing is directly associated with this bubble—which is at once the guide, the indicator, and the critic of your performance. The idea is to move that cutting surface—the bubble—equally back and forth across the bevel. The

Fig. 5-3 Running water onto the horizontal smoothing stone before using it. The stone should be soaked with water, but it should not have such a film that grinding will be impossible.

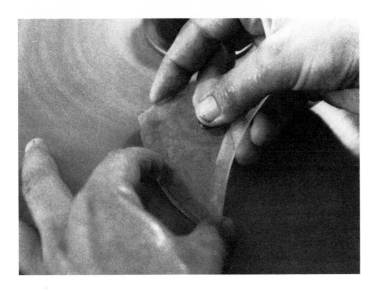

Fig. 5-4 Smoothing an outside curve on the horizontal smoothing stone. The glass has been tipped toward the bottom of the picture.

more evenly you move it, the fewer facets you will end up with. To get the bubble to move and flow evenly under the bevel area, you must lift up the edges of the glass. You should practice doing this.

Remember, this is the wheel that causes all those facets (or the majority of them) that we have been referring to right from the start. Facets are caused at the point of glass removal. They are caused by the bubble pausing in its shuttle to a greater or lesser extent. A very short pause, a slight tilting of the glass even for a split second, is enough to cause a facet. It is frustrating—especially

Fig. 5-5 The proper angle at which the beveled edge is held against the horizontal smoothing stone. Since the wheel is rotating clockwise, this is working "with the wheel" rather than "against the wheel."

Fig. 5-6 On a difficult piece to hold onto while smoothing, put your finger on the edge of the glass in the direction of the spin of the wheel. This way the glass can't get away from you.

at first—to continue with an activity that seems to be working against itself. However, as you persevere, you will find that the movement of the bubble becomes fairly second nature. It is all in the positioning of the glass against the surface of the wheel.

What you must learn to do is to pull down on the angle until you see the bubble going from edge to edge of your bevel, rocking the glass back and forth at the same time. The bubble all but disappears when it comes to the edge of the mitre. Watch your pressure, and try to keep it as constant as you can. Remember, this wheel has a tremendous amount of drag, so use less pressure

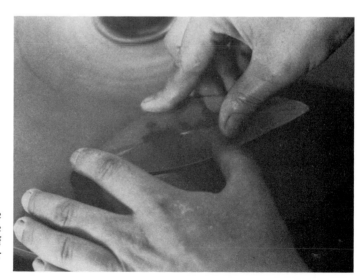

Fig. 5-7 Smoothing a feather shape on the horizontal stone. It must be held tightly here so that the drag of the stone doesn't take it out of your hands.

Fig. 5-8 Smoothing the feather shape on a vertical smoothing wheel. The piece is being rocked down toward the upper surface of the wheel, as shown, and the reverse motion should follow instantly.

than you did on the roughing wheel until you get used to the feel of this one.

When you first start with the smoothing stone, it is a good idea to practice on some waste bevels until you begin to get a "hand sense" of the character of this wheel. After you have become more or less accustomed to the drag—and it can be a shock at first, some beginners actually having their glass snatched from their hands by it—then go ahead and apply your roughed pieces. Use a moderate pressure to remove the sand. Then, to remove any facets that you might have caused, do a feather smoothing. This is a light, fast smoothing, and since it is, or will become, one

Fig. 5-9 Smoothing the edge of a polished bevel.

of the major factors in your technique with this stone, it is a good idea to get into practice with it at the beginning.

As you start to smooth, don't concentrate on any particular sandy areas. Just keep working over the entire surface of the bevel. This will get you to these areas as a part of the whole. Again, this advice is to prevent you from causing facets by concentrating too much on a particular region of the bevel. As you go along smoothing your surface you will see that it begins to flatten any slight belly—or uneven surface—it may have brought from the cast-iron stone. If you have a ridge or other uneven surface, you will notice that when the bubble gets to that place it will deform. It can split or elongate or twist. As you work your surface on the stone, the surface of the glass will become flat and your bubble will become bigger and wider. If it deforms, it means it is not fully contacting the glass and the stone at that high point. The bubble is quick to tell you what your glass surface is like.

Hints for Smoothing

1. You want to remove *all* the sand, not just most of it.

2. Try to keep the pressure of both hands even. Most workers tend to lean more with one hand than the other. Watch the bubble as an indication of this.

3. When you are finished with this wheel, you should try to have all the sand out and also as many facets as possible. The cork wheel, the next station, takes much longer to remove facets than does the smoothing stone, so don't count on it to do the work that you should be doing now.

4. Learn new rhythms with the bubble. Learn to correct an untrue surface by bringing the bubble halfway down several times, and then allowing it to run the entire length every so often to make sure you aren't causing a new facet as you correct the old one.

5. Be careful of the corners. These are danger spots, as you might have guessed. If a corner begins to grow, send the bubble into it less, maybe only every three or four times as you shuttle the bubble over the rest of the surface. Keep tipping the glass.

6. Consider the smoothing stone technique—tipping the glass—as similar to those puzzles where you tilt the board to move little steel balls into holes or down corridors. You develop a hand sense for it after a while, no matter how awkward you were at first. Tipping the glass against the smoothing stone will also become second nature after a while.

7. Remember that corners do tend to move. While you can keep putting them back to some extent, if this process is allowed to continue, eventually you will get distortion in these areas. If a corner angle has moved, just go to the contiguous surface and push it back. The trick is to do this while removing as little glass as possible. Natural light is best for checking your angles.

8. It is a good idea when looking down your mitred angle for flaws to cover the corners with your fingers. Otherwise the bevel

Fig. 5-10 Harry Bullock of Prism Glass smoothing an extra-long piece of glass on its roughed edge. The IB–16 smoothing stone protrudes enough above the rim of the metal splash pan to make this possible. The glass still must be tipped and worked one area at a time, just as with a smaller piece.

Fig. 5-11 A large piece of glass can be smoothed at the horizontal station of the IB–16 so long as you stay above the outer metal rim. Enough of the stone and the cast-iron plate protrudes above this rim to allow the process. You will be using the outer edges of both the stone and the cast-iron wheel, tipping the glass toward the floor. We wouldn't advise handling a much larger sheet of glass than the one shown, however.

Fig. 5-12 Smoothing a 1″ bevel, the size called for by the size of the glass. (Courtesy The Glass Bevel.)

could appear to be bowed. It could be an optical illusion. You don't want to spend time trying to correct this.

9. Pressure is definitely a deciding factor in the smoothing stone technique. We distinguish between very strong, moderate, and feather pressure. We once had one student who was so strong that he could forcefully press the glass against the stone and get the bubble to go all the way down the length of the bevel. He didn't have to do any tipping. This is far more pressure than the average person can apply. If we tried it (and we did), we would be totally worn out after making a single side of a single bevel. However, it is also true that your hands do get strong from beveling (as from milking, although that's a different angle).

10. For practice, try purposely to make a facet just to see how they are formed. This will help you understand more fully what might at first appear to be a somewhat abstract defect. To make a facet, just hold the glass in one spot against the stone. It won't take long for you to develop a good one. Then practice getting rid of it, first using light pressure, then feather pressure.

11. Facets usually come in corners because corners are the stopping and starting points for the movement of the bubble. Also, most workers tend to treat the corners gingerly, since they are attempting not to overshoot them. To get rid of these corner facets, give these areas a light, fast smoothing. Don't give the bubble a chance to pause long enough to cause another facet. Then, every so often, feather-smooth the entire surface: That is, shoot the bubble across the surface as fast as possible. The lighter the touch of the glass against the stone, the faster the bubble can move. Practice this touch, which should be as delicate as you can apply. Here you should almost be able to feel the water flowing between the glass and the stone.

12. Men have a harder time than women in feather smoothing because they tend to use too much pressure. They often find that a strong pressure is more easily projected, and at first they may think they will get the smoothing done more rapidly in this way. However, feather smoothing is just as essential whether you press forcefully or moderately at first. The facets still will form. Another problem with overpressure is loss of control. This can ruin an entire bevel.

13. Take a break when your hands begin to feel the strain.

Keeping Your Stone Lubricated

The only lubrication or coolant used on the smoothing stone is water. This rule applies to both natural sandstone and aluminum oxide stones.

The amount of water you have flowing on the wheel will depend on how fast you want to remove glass, as opposed to how much you want to ease the drag, or pull, of the wheel on your glass.

In other words, a smaller amount of water dripping on your wheel will speed cutting but increase drag. (This sounds a bit like flying lessons rather than beveling lessons.) The opposite is also true: a greater amount of water will make it much simpler to hold the glass against the stone, but the smoothing process will take a lot longer, as the glass is really riding on a cushion of water rather than bearing directly against the grinding surface of the stone.

In time, you will find a happy medium between the cutting speed and the amount of drag you want to put up with. Or decide to take flying lessons instead.

If your stone surface is not sufficiently wet—or, as can happen, you start to use it, forgetting to turn on the water at all—you will quickly be reminded of your lapse by the fires that will appear between the stone and glass. These are quick flashes, not quite sparks, that will do no harm to stone or glass if the process is not extended unduly. There is, of course, no reason it should be. What it does is remind you that the stone surface is not wet. Don't be embarrassed if this happens to you; we have all had this particular memory lapse.

Dressing the Stone

We use the word *dressing* to mean correcting an out-of-round or out-of-flat condition. We do not use it in the sense of "cleaning," and it should not be used with that in mind. Dressing means changing the shape of a stone or a wheel—in other words, getting it into the shape that is optimal for working with that particular station.

Dressing is done differently for different wheels. The cast-iron wheel, for example, will become out of flat about in the center because this is where it is used the most. When this happens, you must take it to a machine shop to have it reflattened. That is all you can do with this wheel; there's no way you can fix it yourself.

A new cast-iron wheel will last the average hobbyist—and even the average craftsman who bevels for a living—practically forever. If you have purchased a used machine, one with perhaps many miles of beveling on it, you may have to have the cast-iron wheel redressed eventually. But, even here, it is hardly a common occurrence. A more likely reason for having to redress this wheel is some sort of accident, such as something heavy falling on it. It is a good idea not to use the horizontal wheels of your beveling machine as catchall tabletops when you aren't beveling. Such indifference to these surfaces, under the impression that they are indestructible, can cost you money.

If you want to dress either sandstone or aluminum oxide wheels, you must have a special dressing machine. The machine has a diamond tip within a graduated holder that runs back and forth over the wheel. This corrects an out-of-flat condition by removing portions of the stone to compensate. On horizontal wheels you usually correct for an out-of-flat condition and on vertical wheels for an out-of-round condition.

As an individual beveler, it is unlikely that you would have a dressing machine. You can still dress the sandstone wheel yourself, but it is not something you would want to do for fun. You will probably need help, such as two more strong people, about eight hours of time, 2′ × 4′ metal bars, and Carborundum. It is also possible to build a dressing machine, which isn't difficult but takes time. However, is it worth it? How many times will you have to dress a wheel back to its true condition? The answer for most of us is practically never. Rather than building a machine, it is much easier and more civilized to send the wheel back to the factory. If you want to be a totally self-sufficient in-house operation, you can get a dressing attachment for the IB–16, and possibly for other machines as well.

What you should keep in mind, more than the specifics of dressing, is that these wheels sometimes do go out of "true." It depends on the age of the wheels, the amount of work you do, and the care you take with them.

Both the aluminum oxide and the sandstone wheel are solid all the way through. They should last for hundreds of hours. One trick in caring for these wheels is to use the whole surface rather than using the surface continually in one spot. If you make a habit of this, these surfaces will last almost indefinitely, since the wheels will continue to function all the way through to the core. The less you have to dress any wheel, the better, since by using the whole surface of the wheel you are dressing as you use it. Every time you have to machine-dress the wheel, you remove some of the surface to get to the lowest point, which is the area that has suffered continual use. Constant machine dressing of course makes the wheel smaller and smaller.

Cleaning the Sandstone

Cleaning stones involves removing various contaminants from the surface, particularly glass particles. The sandstone wheel tends to glaze after a time from the grinding process. To a certain extent, this glazing can be helpful. Once the wheel forms a glaze, it cuts or grinds more smoothly than before. It doesn't grind quite as fast as before, but you might want to overlook the additional time spent for the soft quality of the smooth surface.

The smoothing wheel works well when it has a certain amount of glaze on it. However, if too much glaze builds up, the grinding will be too slow. What you have to do then is break the glaze. The easiest way to do this is to pass a piece of emery cloth over the surface of the wheel while it is running dry with no water. This will effectively remove all the glaze, or, if you are careful, leave just enough to continue to provide that nice satin finish to the glass. Emery cloth is so fine that you can't apply too much pressure and change the shape of the wheel in any way. Obviously you don't want to dress the wheel while cleaning it. You can easily tell when the glaze is removed by the loss of the shiny surface and by the more rapid grinding. If we remove all the glaze in the cleaning process, we put some back onto the surface with soft chunk or slab glass. To do this, turn the water on and wait until the cleaned wheel becomes wet. Then pass the soft chunk glass over the surface until you feel enough glaze has been deposited. Not every worker approves of this method, but keep it in mind if only for experimental purposes.

In using emery cloth to clean the stone, you can hold it to the stone by hand (although some uncomfortable friction may develop), or you can wrap it around a block of wood. The length of time that you hold the emery cloth to the wheel depends on how much the wheel needs to be cleaned. If bits of grit from the cast-iron wheel have become partly embedded, you might be able to remove them by hand with a swipe of the emery cloth. In other instances, you might have to hold the emery cloth wrapped in the block of wood to the wheel for fifteen minutes or so. We favor 120-grit or even slightly finer emery cloth for this purpose.

The Vertical Versus the Horizontal Stone

Everything that we have said so far about the smoothing stone applies almost equally to both the horizontal and the vertical ones. There are some practical differences, however. For one thing, it is easier to do the work on the horizontal stone. We find that it takes almost double the time to do the same amount of work on the vertical stone. For another, the horizontal stone is more flexible so far as making corrections for facets and mitres. However, the vertical stone takes up less space, and since it is smaller, it is less expensive. This is certainly a primary consideration. Furthermore, the vertical stone can do any shape the horizontal can do plus inside curves. These can be done on the horizontal stone, but they are more tricky.

If you are working with a vertical stone, we suggest that you put a bevel on the edge of it as many of the old-timers did. Very often, as many of them have told us, they did the majority of their smoothing of inside curves on that edge. Note that this edge is a flat bevel, not a rounded surface. Essentially what this technique does is to make a narrower smoothing stone, since the surface will be easier for making an inside curve.

If you work on the flat surface of the vertical stone without beveling it—holding the glass inside curve flat against it, ends pointing up and down—you will find that the stone mainly contacts these ends, arriving at the center of the curve after the ends have been ground down. This leaves an uneven finish, to say the least. Thus you lose all the work you put into the bevel.

Of course you wouldn't do this. What you would do, if you want to use the flat surface of the stone, is use the same technique that you used with the vertical diamond. You don't tip and roll your bevel to conform to the shape of the wheel, as you will change the shape of the curve. Again, you will be taking off more at the ends than in the middle.

Keep your working glass area parallel to the edge of the wheel. Use moderate pressure at first to remove the sand. Once you have done that, do light, fast feather smoothing, just as you would on the horizontal stone. Many beginners worry more about where to stand when they use the vertical wheel than they do with the horizontal one. We find that, like the diamond wheel, it is best to stand parallel to the wheel, not directly in front of it. For some people it takes much more pressure on the vertical stone to remove the sand from the bevel than on the horizontal one. Standing correctly will save time by allowing you to exert this extra pressure. You should maintain a smooth motion, remembering to keep turning the glass so that the surface being ground is always parallel to the rim of the wheel.

Hints for the Vertical Stone

1. If you are fighting the wheel, you are probably using too much pressure.

2. Learn the proper sound of the wheel when you use optimum pressure. If the wheel is tugging on your glass, lighten up on the pressure.

3. Remember that the mitre can be moved a little bit back at the corner angles to the proper position. But keep in mind that when you move a mitre, you are still removing glass.

4. Before you worry about the mitres, remove all the sand. If you worry about too much at once, you will go around in circles. Only the wheel should do that.

5. Don't try to get the same quick, chattering technique on the vertical wheel as you do on the horizontal to get the mitred angles where they should be. Here the technique is mainly to push, push, push the mitred angles into place a little at a time. On the horizontal stone you could quickly pick up and drop one of the sides of the glass to move the opposite angle. On the vertical stone this is much too awkward.

6. Oddly enough, if you don't concentrate too much on the mitred angles, they will usually find their own positioning fairly accurately. This is especially true if you keep the edge of the glass being ground parallel to the rim of the wheel. In this instance, the mitre has no choice but to go where it belongs. If you overturn the glass on the wheel, the mitre will go beyond where it should be. The opposite occurs when you underturn—that is, if you go either less than or more than parallel with the grinding surface to the rim of the wheel.

7. One problem that is greater with the vertical wheel than with the horizontal one is widening of the bevel. Watch the pressure. If you have a lot of sand to remove, you want to use a lot of pressure. But you have to watch that while removing sand you aren't permitting your bevel to overshoot its mitred margins.

8. You will have more control over the glass if you use both hands rather than one hand. You could use one hand for feather pressure, though.

9. When pushing the mitred angles into position, make sure that you come back occasionally over the entire surface of the bevel to smooth it. Otherwise you will end up with a facet where

you moved the mitre. If you have inaccurate mitred angles, you may have to push the angle all the way onto the contiguous surface, then come back from there. This is not a good method to follow routinely. You may end up with a mitre and no glass if you keep going back and forth.

10. If you have beveled the edge of your vertical wheel, you have two options. If you have an inside curve wide enough to fit the face of the wheel, use that because you can obtain contact with the wheel all along the surface, not just at the two ends. (Note: the inside curve is always held vertically with the wheel, not horizontally to it.) If you have an inside curve that is too radical for the surface of the wheel, so that it contacts only on the two ends and not in the middle, use the dressed edge of the wheel.

11. If you want to dress the edge of your vertical stone—put a bevel on it—use a Carborundum dressing stick. This will give you the appropriate flat surface.

12. As with the horizontal stone, the bubble is your guide when you use the vertical stone. The bubble should be steady and should travel the full length of the bevel up and down. The final pressure on both horizontal and vertical stones should be so light that you only touch the facets and not the bevel itself.

13. When you are doing small pieces of glass, it is better to use the vertical stone because it is easier to hold on to the glass. With large pieces of glass, it is faster and more comfortable to use the horizontal stone. You always have more surface touching here.

14. On the vertical stone you have to move the glass fairly quickly or it will tend not only to facet but also to scallop, since there is less glass surface touching than with the horizontal.

Contamination

Be careful not to carry over any grit from the cast-iron wheel to the smoothing stone because it will cause scratches in the glass. If this occurs, however, you can go back to the smoothing stone from the next step, the polishing wheels. True, this will deposit either pumice or cerium oxide on the surface of the smoothing stone, but because these compounds are of a finer grit than the smoothing stone itself, no harm will be done. Both pumice and cerium oxide tend to splash a lot, whereas the roughing and smoothing stations are much cleaner. As we shall see, contamination from compounds can affect not only the various stations but also the worker.

If your smoothing stone becomes contaminated with silicon carbide, or with anything that is scratching your glass, you can clean up quickly with a squeegee or a piece of soft slab or chunk glass. The slab glass will also glaze your wheel while cleaning it. Run it back and forth with the water on.

The Shapes So Far

1. *The square.* The sides of the square are smoothed preferably on the horizontal stone, where a good tipping action can achieve a nice bubble. If you have only a vertical stone, there is no reason

why you can't use it. Just hold a small part of glass surface against it at a time and keep the edge of the glass parallel to the rim of the wheel. Once you get used to the technique, you will have little difficulty.

2. *The shield.* Smoothing and roughing outside curves can be difficult. On the vertical wheel the bubble should be steady and travel the full length of the bevel up and down as you roll the glass up and down on that curve. Learn to do the curve smoothly to avoid facets. Remove the sand with a good pressure, then lighten the pressure so that you can go faster. Go as fast as you can to remove the facets without losing control.

The trick on outside curves is to develop a hand sense for changing that turn and keeping the angle as you make the curve in a fluid, nonhesitating manner. This is true on both horizontal and vertical stones. It is easy to put facets into an outside curve, especially if you turn too slowly on the stone.

3. *The circle.* A circle is difficult because it has all those stopping and starting points. Many circles have the same facets as those in the shield, but they are in a more or less regular pattern around the circumference and thus can look as though they are part of a design.

If your facets have smooth areas in between them in an outside curve, you can probably smooth them down completely on the cork wheel. But if they are throughout the bevel, you must remove them on the smoothing wheel. These would be too much for the cork wheel to handle.

4. *The star.* The preferred wheel for the star is the vertical one. If you have only a horizontal wheel, you will have to practice using the edge of it to smooth inside curves. This takes practice, but it certainly can be done. Some workers who have a horizontal smoothing stone also have a vertical one, a cone wheel. However, not everyone who has a vertical setup by itself (as with the Denver Studio Model Beveler) will also have a horizontal wheel.

Ideally, you can do complete bevels on any of these combinations, or, more practically, on a single-type setup with only one wheel for each station. Here the vertical stone is the more flexible stone because of its almost unique capacity for inside curves and its ability to adapt to all other shapes if you have to make a choice of one.

Seaming on the Stone

We came across this technique in Chapter 4 when we spoke of smoothing the glass blank on the cast-iron wheel to get a smooth edge (see Figs. 4-15, 4-25, and 4-26). During the roughing process, you may get more chips on the edge of the glass. You don't want to reseam this edge on the cast-iron wheel, since it will take off too much of this thin surface. However, you don't have that problem on the stone. You would seam this edge here so that later, during the polishing process, the chips on the edge will not splinter further or crack the glass all the way across.

The seaming is done all the way across the edge of the bevel. In this process the edge of the glass is directly flat against the stone wheel. This seals or closes off these chipped areas. Even if you see no chipping, it is a good idea to do this routinely on any beveled edges that are to be exposed, such as the edges of coffee tables or free-hanging decorations. Then when people look at your finished work, they will get the point, not the edge.

CHAPTER 6

Interlude: A Clinic on Roughing and Smoothing

Having come this far, it might be time to sit back and digest the first five chapters. One way to gain a good perspective on techniques and principles is to see them through the eyes of other workers. Their questions could be your own. They may be phrased differently and given a slightly individual emphasis, but perhaps they will bring out facets (if we may use the term) that will recapitulate your own ideas.

Or you might use this interlude to bevel a few quick pieces.

Questions and Answers

The roughing stage is where the shape of your bevel takes place. It is here where the steepness of the angle and width of the bevel are decided. Both of these are personal preferences. However, there are some guidelines to follow.

Q: What angle am I trying to achieve in beveling?

A: The steepness of the angle will depend greatly on the thickness of the glass to be beveled. Suppose we're talking about $\frac{1}{4}''$ plate with a standard $\frac{1}{2}''$ bevel. The angle will be much *less* than if you use $\frac{3}{8}''$ plate or $\frac{1}{2}''$ plate. The angle also changes by lessening or widening the width of the bevel. It can also be determined by the amount of glass removed. Say we make a $\frac{1}{2}''$ bevel, leaving $\frac{1}{8}''$ on the edge. This angle will be much less than if we left only an edge of $\frac{1}{16}''$. So, while the angle you achieve depends on you, the thickness of the glass and the steepness of the bevel modify your choice.

Q: How thick or thin should I leave the edge?

A: No thicker than $\frac{1}{8}''$ or thinner than $\frac{1}{16}''$. An edge that is much thicker than $\frac{1}{8}''$ won't fit in the came. If it is much thinner than $\frac{1}{16}''$, it could be weak and fracture either upon polishing or during assembly.

Q: If I have a ridge in my bevel, is it okay to leave it and depend on the second step to remove it?

A: No. That is a bad habit to get into. It will take half the time to remove this edge on the diamond wheel simply because your stone wheel is a finer grit. You should make a practice of doing the best possible job on each wheel before moving on to the next one. The next wheel has enough of its own work to do without also having to make up the deficiencies of the station before it.

Q: I have the 4″ by 1½″ diamond wheel. I can do very small bevels with it, and I think I can also do larger bevels too. Why should I even buy the 8″ wheel?

A: Simply because of the slighter radius of the wheel, you will have a smaller amount of the wheel touching your larger piece of glass. This will cause ridges and faceting.

Q: I have an instruction manual that states: "Have the glass at a 30-degree angle on the wheel." I don't have an eye for angles and find it difficult to determine just how to begin.

A: A good starting angle is simply set: Just put the lower edge of your glass against the wheel (Fig. 6-1). With each trip across

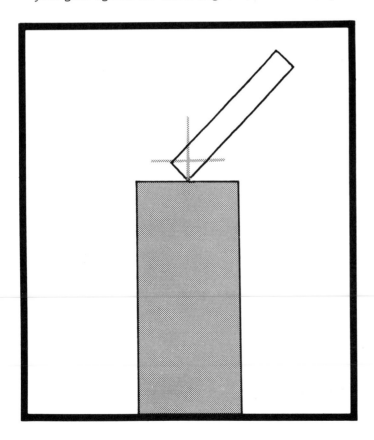

Fig. 6-1 Placing lower edge of glass against the wheel.

the wheel, you will be slowly widening your bevel by lessening the angle of the glass against the wheel. It's that easy.

The aluminum oxide stone removes the abrasive surface left from the roughing stage. It, in turn, leaves a smooth but hazy surface that can be polished. This wheel takes the most time and requires the most skill to produce a premium bevel.

Q: Why is my smoothing stone leaving a very rough, almost scratchy surface?

A: A new stone wheel, until it is broken in and partially glazed, will tend to cut up rough. When glass is fed onto this wheel, it produces a glaze on the surface. Glazing the stone wheel can be accomplished after only a few hours use. After this has been done, you will notice a much quieter contact on the wheel and a smoother surface. If you clean your stone after several hours' use, you must reglaze the wheel. You can do this by running a small piece of slab glass across the surface. This works well both to glaze and clean the wheel of debris.

Q: I've managed to contaminate my stone wheel with some grit from the cast-iron wheel. What do I do now?

A: Relax. This happens no matter how careful you think you are being. A piece of emery cloth and water should clear your wheel surface quickly.

Q: I work in my basement, which has no natural light. How can I find facets with artificial light?

A: In lighting the bevel for facets in the absence of natural light, place direct light in a position lower than your head. Light at that level or slightly lower will reflect down onto the glass and reveal the facets. You will, admittedly, have as hard a time finding them when you hold the glass against the direct light as you would with daylight.

Q: I have trouble getting a wide bubble on the stone wheel. Why?

A: Your bubble, or cutting surface, will contact on a high spot. If you haven't removed glass evenly on the diamond wheel, an uneven surface occurs. Go back to the diamond wheel and reflat the surface.

Q: I have removed all the sand, but I still have a wavy, faceted surface. What causes this?

A: When you use normal pressure and move the glass slowly on the wheel, do you notice the bubble bouncing? With every bounce, a facet occurs. After removing the sand, do a very light, fast smoothing, one that will not allow the bubble to stay in one spot long enough to cause a facet. Facets are more likely to occur in the corners of your bevel next to the mitre simply because this is a starting and stopping point. The bubble flows more smoothly at the center of the bevel than in the corners. A light, fast smoothing will solve or at least ease your facet problem.

Q: What causes scratches from the stone wheel?

Fig. 6-2 Doing inside and outside curves on the diamond wheel.

A: If your wheel has been broken in, then it could be one of two things: (1) too much pressure, or (2) something has contaminated your wheel, probably from the sponge under the wheel. Clean the sponge and the wheel.

Q: My stone wheel bounces back and forth slightly. Why?

A: The labels on the sides of your wheel can cause this. If parts of them have peeled off, remove what is left. Now check the wheel for a bounce. Another possibility is that the lead lining in the center of the wheel has been damaged by forcing the wheel onto the shaft. Take care to ease your vertical stone wheel onto the shaft by turning it, not hitting it, into position.

Q: What is a perfect bevel?

A: A perfect bevel is as clear and undistorted as the untouched surface of the glass. We have never seen one, but this is a goal to strive for.

Q: Why do my inside- and outside-curve bevels tend to be straight and very thin on the ends and thick in the middle?

A: You must turn your glass on the diamond wheel. Make sure that you turn your glass so that its edge is kept parallel to the edge of the wheel (Fig. 6-2). Remember, you are always beveling to the same shape as the edge of your piece. If you keep the grinding surface parallel to the rim of the wheel, you will easily keep your beveled edge the same thickness all around and your mitre even in width. In short, this method assures you of removing glass evenly.

Q: How wide a bevel can I make on my beveling machine?

A: We suggest that you make it no wider than your wheel.

Q: How long a piece can I make on my beveling machine?

A: With some practice, there is almost no limit. Practically, you can make as long a piece as you can hold and control easily.

Q: After I roughed my piece, I noticed a big cut or ridge on one side. What happened?

A: Somewhere in the process, you moved the glass off the edge of the wheel. Fix it by removing more glass so as to get below it.

Q: I can't seem to form a sharp mitre in the corner of my bevel. Why is this?

A: Check the edge of your glass. You have probably removed so much glass that there's not enough left to form your mitre. Alas, you must start over.

Q: How do I know when my diamond wheel needs to be dressed?

A: When you first begin to notice that you have to apply more pressure to achieve a speedy cut. Make sure to dress your wheel wet, using approximately one-third of your dressing stick. Proper care of your wheel will prolong its life.

Q: My diamond wheel bounces back and forth. why?

A: Check for three things that could easily cause this: (1) Check your bushing. These are only plastic, so they do wear out. (2) Make sure your locking flange is to the inboard side of your wheel. If your diamond wheel rests against the nut, it will bounce. (3) Make sure your bushing is no wider than your wheel. If it is, the wheel will not turn with the shaft because the flanges have tightened against the bushing and not the wheel.

Q: The mitres on the point of my bevel are off center. Do I have to go back to the diamond wheel? I'm on the stone wheel now.

A: No. Since you moved them on the stone wheel, you can rely on it to move them back into position. Remember, your stone is removing glass. So, as you move them, many changes can take place in these angles as well as in the bevel. This is one reason why the smoothing stage takes the most practice and skill to come out with a good bevel.

Q: My diamond wheel has a side-to-side wobble. Is something wrong with the wheel?

A: Check for the following problems: (1) Make sure that you have a bushing inside your wheel. (2) Make sure that you have a flange on both sides of your wheel. If the nut is tightened right to the wheel instead of to the flange, a side-to-side bounce occurs. (3) Tighten your wheel onto the smooth part of the shaft rather than onto the threads. Your wheel won't be centered under the faucet, but it will still be kept sufficiently wet.

Q: For a long time I had very few problems with facets coming off the stone wheel. Now it seems, suddenly, no matter what I do, I get deep facets. What am I doing wrong?

A: If you were successful for a long time and this problem began suddenly, it is probably not your technique that is causing the faceting. It sounds as though your stone wheel needs to be dressed. Check your wheel for an "out-of-round" condition by steadily holding a pencil at the front of the wheel while it is turning. If it is out of round, the pencil will mark only the high spots of the wheel. If your wheel is "out of flat," it is usually visible to the eye. However, this can be checked by placing a straight edge across your wheel while holding a light behind it. If light shows under the straight edge, your wheel should be dressed flat.

Q: I have been doing quite a bit of wheel engraving, especially star cuts. My 6″ by $\frac{1}{2}$″ stone wheel holds its shape for a few bevels after I dress it to a point. Is there any other type of wheel that I can use? I just can't keep dressing the wheel after only a few bevels.

A: We have been aware of this problem for some time and have been testing other wheels for hardness. We find that aluminum oxide is still the best composition. However, a denser, harder wheel is needed to avoid the constant dressing. Denver Machinery has a new 6″ by $\frac{1}{2}$″ stone that fits this description and is now available. We tried it, and it took us thirty minutes to dress this wheel to a point in comparison with fifteen minutes on our old stone. This alone says something for this new stone's hardness. We had approximately fifteen hours' use on this stone before a very light dressing was needed to sharpen the point. One of these new wheels may solve your problem.

Q: My diamond wheel is rather dull even after I have dressed it with the silicon carbide stick. Do you have any other suggestions? The wheel is only eight months old.

A: Try flipping your wheel around on the shaft. If it has been used in only one direction, both sides of the diamond haven't been used. If you have already done this and the diamond is still dull, your wheel is obviously worn out. It can wear out in eight months with constant use, or it can last for two years with occasional use.

Q: My machine worked fine for several weeks. One day I turned it on and it bounced and vibrated. After a few minutes it stopped. What happened?

A: We have had this very thing happen when we have forgotten to remove the sponge from under the stone wheel. Overnight the wheel soaked up the water from the sponge, making one side of the wheel heavier than the other. The wheel soon dries out, and the machine will then run smoothly. This is what seems to have happened with yours. This same situation can also occur with the felt wheel. Just remember, when you finish for the day, remove the sponge and recheck to make sure that all faucets are turned off tightly.

Q: I have an older-model Denver Studio Model machine. Recently, I compared the performance of my machine to a newer model. I noticed that mine vibrates more. What improvements have been made to ease this vibration since my machine was built?

A: Denver Machinery gave this answer: "Our new machine in the Studio Model has an antivibration kit, which can also be ordered for the older model. The kit bolts the bottom plywood to plywood resting right under the arbors. This pulls the arbors down tightly, reducing the vibration."

Q: I have owned a Denver Studio Model for about a year. I have been satisfied with it, but I now find that I have enough business to warrant buying a larger machine, one with horizontal wheels. I realize that it takes a different technique to bevel on these wheels compared to the vertical ones I am used to. The question is, What can I do with my old machine when I buy a new one? Is there another use for it, or should I simply try to sell it? Frankly, it has been such a good companion, I hate to get rid of it.

A: Well, cheer up. You don't have to. If you want another Denver machine, we suggest the IB–16. This model is made for people who already have the Studio Model. All straight and outside curves can be done on this larger machine, and you can do all inside curves and wheel engraving on your Studio Model. The Studio Model takes up so little space that it is no problem having two machines. And you can keep it set up for only roughing and smoothing inside curves. One side can hold your 8" and

4″ stones, and the other side can hold your 8″ and 4″ diamonds. This reduces the time spent in changing wheels for tighter curves. Whatever large machine you do get, we strongly suggest that you keep your Studio Model. You never know when it will come in handy. We certainly wouldn't be without ours.

Q: I'd like some information about polishing that will . . .

A: Hold on, just a minute. Please read the next two chapters first.

CHAPTER 7

The Third Station: Semipolishing

The purpose of semipolishing is to remove the haze that has been left on the surface of the glass by the smoothing stone. Ideally, at this stage all facets should have been removed as well as all the sand, every last grain of it. Now you are ready to semipolish with either of the two wheels that can be used for the job: the cork wheel and the fiber wheel.

The Notion of Semipolishing

In addition to removing the haze from the bevel, semipolishing removes any defects that occurred in the previous two stations. However, you might get quite a high polish from the cork wheel. Many of the old-time bevelers did just this; in fact, they got such a high polish that they stopped the beveling process at the cork station, thus saving time and money. We do not want to do this, and that is the main reason why we make the distinction between semipolishing and high polishing. Each step in the beveling process contributes to the final product, and to attempt to combine any two stages into one invariably diminishes this final product in some way, even though it may be subtle. Since you have gone to a lot of trouble up to and through this stage in the process, it seems ridiculous, if we may coin a phrase, to cut corners now. Our advice is not to use this third station in any way as a final one. When you finish the fourth station and compare the end result with the end result of the cork station, you will see why. So keep the cork and fiber wheels as another step, not the final one. Your bevels will be happier, and so will you.

The Cork Wheel

The cork wheel is a vertical wheel, and it is made of real cork. Cork has been found to be the best material for the purpose. Leather has been tried as a substitute, but it was found wanting. The cork on the wheel will last indefinitely unless you cut into it with your glass. Both the cork and felt wheels (the final station) can be nasty to work because they are extremely messy. On the

Denver Model IB–16, the cork and felt wheels are in the center of the vertical section. They are larger than the diamond and stone wheels, and you will notice that they are set to a different speed: They turn much more slowly. The main reason for this is to give them more of a chance to hold the various compounds on their surface; the faster these wheels spin, the more they throw the compounds at you. This tendency is already uncomfortably accurate, even with the slower rate of spin of the wheels. On the IB–16 it is possible to use a specific motor so that the polishing wheels can be individualized. On the Denver Studio Model Beveler, where only a single motor is used, all the wheels spin rapidly. This is necessary for roughing and smoothing so the process doesn't take forever. A cork wheel on this machine would be impossible; it would spin so rapidly that it would throw off the compound immediately. That is why the fiber wheel is used instead.

Pumice and the Cork Wheel

The cork wheel, unlike the felt wheel, is not porous. This makes it more difficult to keep the compound on its surface than with the felt wheel. It also explains why it "spits" more than the felt wheel does. Knowing why it does this may not help you keep your temper, however. Especially when working with the cork wheel, protect your clothing and your work area. It isn't silly even to consider wearing a raincoat, and certainly you should wear goggles to avoid getting pumice in your eyes. The average RPMs of the large felt and cork on the IB–16 is 225, compared with the 400 RPMs of the smaller, outside wheels. You can make the wheels spin more slowly by putting different size pulleys on the machine, but few workers we know go to this extreme. Besides, you don't want to slow these wheels down too much or you will be spending more time with them. Accept them for what they are; you will get used to them.

The felt and cork wheels go onto the machine without prior dressing. Only stones must be dressed before they are placed. Dressing of cork and felt wheels takes place (when necessary) directly on the beveler. A dressing machine isn't needed.

The cork wheel can straighten out a number of problems, such as getting rid of minor scratches, removing deep haze, and even removing some final specks of sand. But the wheel can cause some problems as well. You can soften your mitres by running over the break lines of the bevel, and you can get pumice lines.

Pumice comes in powder form. To use it in beveling, you add water to make it into a paste. We use a half-and-half mixture. There are various grits of pumice, from fine to coarse. We use the extra-coarse variety since it removes some sand and many facets. No matter how careful you are, you may still find sand and facets in the bevel even after the most judicious use of the smoothing stone. Fine-grit pumice takes forever to get an effect.

The pumice lines that result from using extra-coarse pumice are a problem. These are striations parallel to the glass in the bevel, and you will probably end up with a certain number of them no matter how careful you are. But since each wheel can be counted on to remove the blemishes added by the wheel before, you can remove them with the felt wheel.

The cork wheel is never used by itself; it is always used with the pumice paste applied to it. The effect on the glass is the combination of the cork and the pumice, not the influence of either alone. We use a sponge to apply the pumice to the wheel. You can do this either with the wheel running or at a standstill, turning it by hand. It depends how much patience you have at the moment. Some workers use a paintbrush to apply their pumice, but we find this tedious in the extreme. Also, the paintbrush seems to work only with a thinner mix of pumice and water, and this is ineffective for polishing. All told, a sponge is best. Apply the pumice as you turn the wheel by hand until the wheel becomes whitish (or until your hair does, if the wheel is spinning as you apply it).

It is a good idea to stand to the side of the wheel rather than in front of it to avoid being splashed by the compound. This is also the case with the felt wheel. The wheel spin is upward for several reasons. Safety is a primary one. If you catch the edge of your glass in the wheel, the glass will be thrown upward and away from you if you lose your grasp, rather than directly at you, as would happen if the spin of the wheel were downward. Another reason is that gravity is already drawing your arms down; with the wheel turning up, some of this effect is nullified, and you don't have to fight gravity and the spin of the wheel as well.

The pumice will not only fly about, it will also get under your clothes, in your shoes, in your hair, and up your nose. It is like

Fig. 7-1 Gathering pumice on a sponge before putting it to the cork-wheel surface.

sandblasting in an open area; the sand simply flies. You may want to wear a hat at this wheel to protect your hair. If you are prepared for the pumice, you may find that it isn't that bad after all. But at least be prepared.

Water isn't necessary for the cork wheel. Unless you turn it off completely, it will work against you and wash the pumice from the wheel. Your mixture of pumice and water must be wet enough to adhere to the cork. The water tap on the machine is there only in case you want to put on another type of wheel.

With the cork wheel the technique is that of tipping and rolling. You don't have to be afraid of changing the shape of your bevel with this wheel, since there is not enough grinding power for that to happen. However, if you don't watch out, you can soften the bevel edge if you keep going over the margins. This is especially true of corner mitres, where the wheel will work right up on them if you give it a chance.

The trick, again, is to watch the bubble. Yes, there is a bubble in this process as well. You control the bubble, as with the stone, with the tipping and rolling or rocking motion. You don't have to worry about staying in any one spot too long—you won't cause any facets with this wheel. You can go as slowly as you like. It is comforting to know that in order to cause a facet you would have to stay in the same spot for quite a long time, and even then you would end up with only a very minor facet.

As the part of the wheel you are working on becomes dry, move to another part of the wheel where the surface is wetter. Just slide the glass over. This is simpler and makes more sense than stopping the wheel to apply more pumice.

The polishing movement on the wheel is diagonal. In other words you will be cross-wheel polishing. As you polish, you will get striations running in one direction; turn the glass so that the

The Cork Wheel Technique

Fig. 7-2 Applying the pumice to the cork wheel while it is spinning.

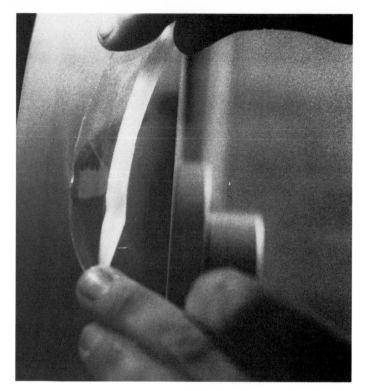

Fig. 7-3 Polishing the feather shape against the cork wheel. Note the bubble three-quarters of the way down. As always, the bubble is your guide. It should stretch all the way across the mitre, as it does here.

striations run crosswise and wipe them out by going at an angle to them. Eventually these striations will become fainter and fainter.

As you use the cork wheel, you will find that most of the haze left from the stone will phase out. This may be dramatic, but getting rid of the haze is not the primary purpose of the cork wheel. Simply to get rid of haze you could go directly from the stone to the felt wheel, the last station. But the purpose of the cork wheel is mainly to remove whatever facets remain from the stone wheel. Once you remove these, you are finished with this wheel, even if you don't feel you have accomplished a full polish. Remember, the cork wheel is a semipolisher.

To avoid softening your mitres, accustom yourself to the sound the cork wheel makes. As you approach a mitre, you can actually hear a change in the sound as the wheel gets to it, not upon it. The sound goes from a smooth tone to a rather rough one. At this point, it is best to stop and go the other way so that you don't lose the sharp mitre line you have worked hard to get. You can also see a difference as well on the bevel as the pumice starts to build up on the side of the mitre. Use this pumice buildup as a stop sign.

The amount of pressure that should be applied to the cork wheel is an individual matter. You must grip the glass fairly tightly

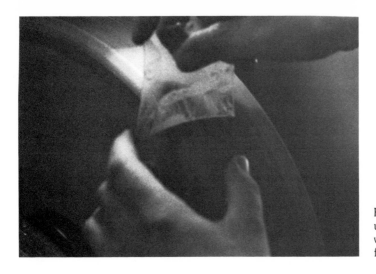

Fig. 7-4 Polishing an inside curve using the rounded edge of the cork wheel. The piece is moved slowly from left to right across that edge.

at the beginning so that the wheel doesn't flip it out of your hands. Pressure against the wheel can be increased if you feel the polishing operation (or defaceting operation) is not going quickly enough. Of course you may not have enough pumice on the wheel in this instance. But assuming you do, you don't want to exert so much pressure that the wheel surface—which is a soft one, compared to the diamond and the stone—grabs the glass and tosses it into the hands of the worker on the other side of the machine. Actually, a caution here: It is never a good idea to stand across from someone using the cork wheel. That mad beveler on the other side could possibly flip you out.

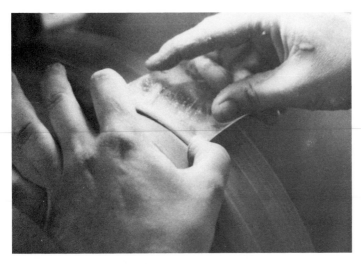

Fig. 7-5 Polishing an inside curve using the surface of the cork wheel. As with the smoothing wheel, you can use a tipping motion for polishing. Turn the piece to the right and then to the left, in addition to tipping, so that you cross-grain, or cross-wheel, polish across the mitre.

Fig. 7-6 Semipolishing the feather shape against the cork wheel. The bubble shows how much tipping is necessary.

Hints for Semipolishing

1. Inside curves can be done on the face of the cork wheel if they don't have radical turns. Again, watch the bubble to make sure you are getting the full effect of the wheel across the bevel. If the curve is too radical for the face of the wheel, go on to the dressed edge of the wheel (see "Dressing the Wheel").

2. If your wheel is turning upward, keep the edge of the glass up to match the turn. If you hold the edge downward, against the turn of the wheel, the surface of the wheel may catch it and flip it out of your hands.

3. More of the wheel's surface touches the bevel when you use the face of the wheel rather than the dressed edge, so use the face of the wheel whenever you can. Remember to use cross-wheel polishing here. Unfortunately, you cannot do this well on an inside curve because the wheel will work right up on the corner bevels. On outside curves you can get away with this technique somewhat better, since you can do a little of the curve at a time. Inside curves can be a problem for cross polishing; you will have to develop your own technique here.

4. The cork wheel tends to dry only on the surface that is being used. Since the wheel holds moisture well, just slide your work over to another area rather than stopping the wheel.

5. If you have a facet or other flaw in the bevel, you can keep working on it, unlike the technique employed with the previous wheels. The cork wheel will not distort the glass.

6. Just because you graduate from one station to the next—as from the stone to the cork—doesn't mean that you can't go back to the stone from the cork if you find it necessary. For instance, there may be so much sand left in the bevel that it would take you days to get it out with the cork. Just go back to the stone. At the same time, you don't want to keep jumping from one wheel to another, so try to get all bevels as perfect as possible at each particular station. Rough them all, then smooth them all, and so on. Mass production saves time.

7. Final defects should be caught at the cork stage. You should not have to go back from the felt station(the final station) to any preceding one. Of course this is possible, but if this happens too often, there is something wrong with your technique at the previous stations. If you don't find out now what you are doing wrong, you will be shuttling back and forth between stations more than you will be working.

8. This third station is the last chance you have to get your mitred angles precisely in line with the glass ones. You can't move them on the last wheel because the grit is too fine. So concentrate on them here.

Dressing the Wheel

You will probably want to dress both the cork and felt wheels to the extent that you modify one rim for inside curves. We find that the best tool for dressing is a heavy-duty rasp. You can use a rasp for the edges of both wheels.

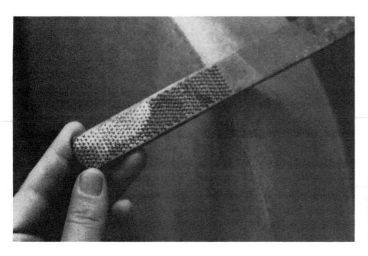

Fig. 7-7 The side of the cork wheel can be rounded to facilitate polishing inside curves and other awkward shapes. This is done with a rasp.

Fig. 7-8 Rounding the cork-wheel edge with the rasp, which must be held firmly.

Filing is done on a dry wheel as it turns. Roll the rasp as you go so that you get a rounded edge on the wheel. Hold the rasp in both hands to obtain maximum control. As you dress the wheel, just touch the surface a little at a time. It is a good idea to use the outside rim of each wheel for dressing rather than the inside rim, which faces the neighboring wheel and is more difficult to get to.

You round off the outside edge of each wheel so that if your inside curve doesn't fit the face of the wheel, it will fit the side. Dressing the wheel will in no way affect its performance, and the bevel will stay on indefinitely. The process allows you to use a single wheel for all sorts of glass shapes, rather than having to buy wheels of different dimensions.

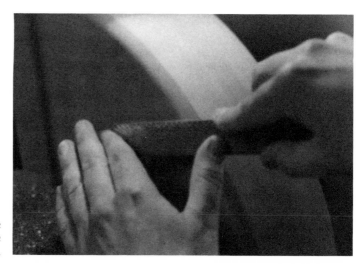

Fig. 7-9 Rounding the edge of the cork wheel for polishing inside curves and other odd-shaped pieces.

Fig. 7-10 The rounded edge on the cork wheel after filing.

You can either round your edge or bevel it. However, although you can round the edge freehand, you need some sort of rest to put a bevel on it. If you want a flat bevel, we suggest at least a $\frac{1}{2}''$ flat surface, but not much over that. A sharp wood chisel is useful here.

Caution: Use a mask when you dress the cork and felt wheels. They produce a great deal of debris in the air, and you don't want to get it in your lungs. The felt wheel is especially bad for dust. The cork produces larger pieces of debris, but there is still a lot of dust. You might use a tool rest to get a good edge.

The Fiber Wheel

It is impossible to use a cork wheel on the small Studio Model Beveler because it won't hold the pumice. Because of the size of this machine, it has a smaller diameter wheel and a faster spin.

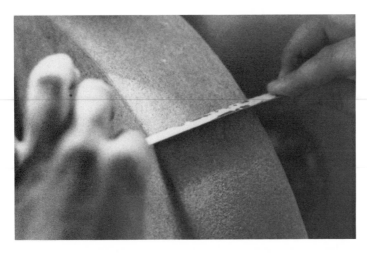

Fig. 7-11 Dressing the cork wheel with the wheel turning. We use a hacksaw blade to roughen up the cork surface. This allows a better contact with the glass.

The fiber wheel was devised as a substitute. The fiber wheel has 600-grit silicon carbide embedded in its Mylar fiber, so no other compound is necessary. However, it does take a lot of water. It also tends to splash this water at you, which puts it right in line with its cousins, the felt and cork wheels.

Before using the fiber wheel, thoroughly soak it in water. Once it is soaked, turn down the water from the spigot. There is no reason to put a sponge under this wheel to cut down on its water-splashing habit, as with other vertical wheels. This wheel will only tear up the sponge and throw the pieces at you. It may also bite your fingers more quickly than any of the other wheels. Therefore, take care when using it and keep your hands to yourself.

As the fiber wheel dries out, it turns a light brown; you must add more water at this point. The fiber wheel will soften the mitres of your bevel much more rapidly than will the cork wheel, so you must be especially careful of these angles. In addition, you have no bubble to use as a guide. All your work must be done by feel. The only hint you have that you are getting too close to a mitred angle is the buildup of water against it. This is a fairly obvious clue once you see what it looks like.

The fiber wheel is softer than the cork wheel, so you must be careful how you apply your glass to it. It will be happy to take the glass out of your hands. The surface of your glass treated by the fiber wheel will look different from a surface treated by cork and pumice. With the cork wheel you do get pumice lines, but the fiber wheel also can leave striations that go even deeper than these. The cork wheel will remove haze from the glass produced

Fig. 7-12 Soft beveling on a pencil bevel. Here the edge of the central mitre of the feather shape is rolled on the cork wheel. Note how blurred it is compared to the sharp edge on regular bevels.

by the smoothing stone. The fiber wheel, if it removes any haze at all, may remove only the deeper variety.

You know when you have finished with this wheel by the absence of facets. This is its main purpose, and for all its idiosyncracies, it is a very forgiving wheel so far as facets are concerned. It gets rid of facets much more rapidly than the cork wheel. When you look at the bevel, you may still see the haze, but the surface will be getting smoother.

This is our favorite wheel for removing facets. We use it constantly for this purpose. It fits both the large and the small Denver machines, and for difficult bevels such as ovals, which tend to accumulate facets at those tight turns, it is just the thing. If you can afford to do so, we suggest adding a step to the beveling protocol and make the progression from diamond, stone, fiber, and cork, to felt. Of course if you have the fiber wheel, you can skip the cork and go directly to the felt to clean up the haze and provide the high polish. The fiber wheel takes some practice to get used to, but we have found it more than worth the effort in the long run.

Soft Beveling

Soft beveling makes your bevel look less rigid and, when done to a purpose, more fluid. In this respect, it can correspond with the overall shape of the glass, which may be only vaguely geometric (see the work of Carl Powell in the color section). Or you may want to leave the glass shape geometric, but without a sharp

Fig. 7-13 Soft beveling completed. The central ridge looks thicker with the light on it because of its rounded surface.

beveled ridge. To this end, soft beveling is done almost exclusively with pencil bevels (see Chapter 10), but we discuss it here because it is accomplished at the semipolishing stage.

The process itself is simple. As one of our students described it, "All you do is make a nice hard ridge and then proceed to foul it up." Well, that is more or less the case. We did this with the feather shape to show the effect (see Fig. 7-13). To soft bevel, roll the break line at the upper surface of the mitre over the cork wheel until you have the rounded edge that you want. You can also start this on the felt wheel if you want a more subtle rounding. The fiber wheel also will round the bevel, although this process can be a little too rapid. You might find it uncontrollable until you practice on a few pieces.

Soft beveling is easy, and when applied to the right design, it is extremely effective, adding an immediate fringe benefit to your technique. Like all effects, it should not be overdone. Nor should it be an accident of technique that you try to get away with. This results in distortion, not design. Its purpose is to get away from the traditional bevel but still retain a beveled identity. Overdone, it becomes just another piece of glass.

CHAPTER 8

The Fourth Station: High Polishing

The fourth wheel is the last stage of the beveling progression. You are now ready for the final transformation of that rather plain if not disreputable piece of scrap plate you started with into an effervescent prism.

The Felt Wheel

The felt wheel, the final wheel, like the cork wheel, is not used alone. Although jeweler's rouge is preferred by some workers, we use cerium oxide with the felt wheel, which we apply with a scrub brush. We turn the machine off during the application process. We like to turn the wheel by hand, although you can do it with the machine on if you wish.

Working with cerium oxide is like dealing with mud pies. As with the cork, you can use a paintbrush to apply the compound, but the scrub brush here is particularly good because the bristles lift up the nap of the felt and work the cerium oxide directly into the surface. Although the felt surface has a pile to it, the cork wheel is smooth. Even on the cork surface, though, a certain amount of roughing is desirable. We sometimes add this with a hacksaw blade held to the surface while the wheel is spinning. With the felt wheel the scrub brush does the job.

Once you have applied the cerium oxide, turn the wheel on and stand out of the way. Cerium oxide flies about even more than pumice; it can easily splatter the ceiling, and it will certainly splatter you.

The Felt Wheel, Water, and Cerium Oxide

Like the cork, the felt is a vertical wheel. Unlike the cork, however, you do use the water spigot on the machine, although you must use it judiciously. If you run the wheel too dry, it will heat the glass and possibly crack it. Since you are working with a water-absorbent material, there is a difference between the wheel running and the wheel standing still. It is okay to have water running on the wheel while it is turning, but once it gets wet and you turn

129

Fig. 8-1 Applying cerium oxide to the felt wheel. This wheel applies the final polish. The scrub brush works the cerium into the nap of the wheel, which will produce a very high polish.

off the machine, all the water in the wheel tends to seep to the bottom. This is a problem because it leaves the surface of the wheel unevenly wet. We avoid this problem by mixing our cerium oxide very wet, putting it on a dry wheel. We use no water from the spigot unless we have a lot of polishing to do and intend to use the wheel almost constantly. If we have trouble achieving the proper amount of water, we may give a few squirts from the spigot while the wheel is turning, but little more than that.

Fig. 8-2A A commercial felt wheel. To save material, the felt does not go to the core of the wheel.

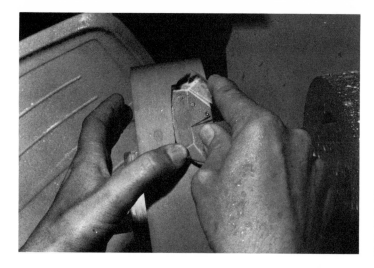

Fig. 8-2B Polishing a small piece
of glass with a short bevel. The ar-
rowlike mark above the right thumb
points to the central bubble, which
guides the polishing.

If you use a sponge to apply the cerium oxide mix to the wheel,
you may find after a while that a thick coating is left on the surface
with little getting into the nap, which is where you want it. If you
polish with the wheel loaded, all you are offering the glass is the
cerium oxide, an inefficient polisher by itself. What you want to
offer is the cerium oxide *plus* the felt. If you don't get the combination of these two against the glass, you can't build up the
proper friction to polish properly. Hence the scrub brush, which
lifts up this thick coating, allowing penetration of the compound
into the material.

It is extremely important that you load the wheel properly because you can't keep an eye on it during the actual process. The
splashing will be so intense that you will be going mostly by feel.

The Technique of Felt-Wheel Polishing

On the felt wheel the glass bevel must become hot from friction
to get rid of the pumice lines. As the glass heats, it can actually
"surface flow." So long as this is wet-hot heat, not dry-hot heat,
the purpose is served nicely. Obviously a dry-hot heat would
fracture the glass. The heat is caused entirely by the friction of felt
and cerium oxide against the glass.

We have noticed that beginners especially tend to polish for
several seconds, then stop, come over to another part of the wheel,
stop, and so forth. Such an erratic rhythm will never build up the
proper friction heat. You should stay on one part of the wheel
and, as with the cork, when it starts to get too dry, slide the glass
over to another section instead of lifting the glass away. This leads
to a continuous polishing, and you can feel the wheel heating
through the glass. The more pressure you apply, the faster you
can polish. It is through continuous polishing that you get rid of
the pumice lines.

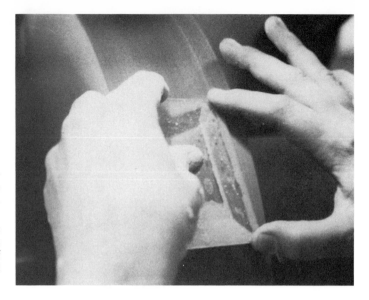

Fig. 8-3 The cleaner you keep your glass, even while doing so messy an operation as polishing, the better you can see what you are doing. This piece is still fairly clean. In a few more minutes it will have to be recleaned. Compare the method of holding the mitre against the wheel with that in Fig. 8-5.

As with the cork wheel, you polish in different directions on the felt wheel. Try to go against whatever striations are on the glass. If the bevel shows polishing grain one way on the cork wheel, on the felt wheel, go in the opposite direction. Always try to cross the grain of the previous wheel.

Since you can't see what you are doing very well, it is a good idea to polish from the middle of the wheel upward so that you don't risk catching your glass. Then turn the glass around to do the remaining surface. Try to remember not to tip the glass too

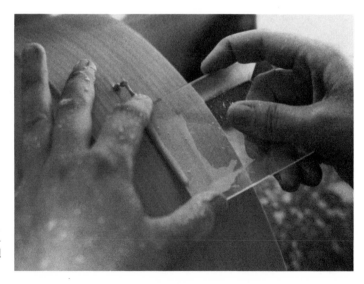

Fig. 8-4 Polishing on the felt wheel. A large buildup of cerium oxide occurs here. The excess must be wiped away periodically.

Fig. 8-5 One way to hold the mitre against the felt wheel for polishing. Compare this with Fig. 8-3. This shows the tipping process that is necessary to get the whole surface of the mitre against the wheel as you polish.

far down the wheel when you turn it around or the wheel may grab it. We try to stay at about the center of the wheel, polishing from the center of the bevel up. Then we turn it around and do the rest. This works quite well. At least we haven't lost any glass lately.

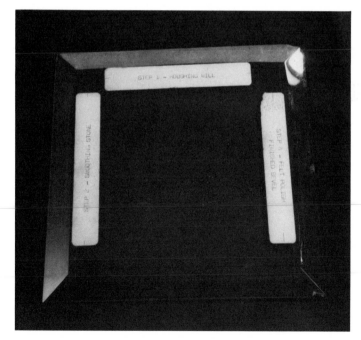

Fig. 8-6 Some beveled surfaces. *Left:* the surface as it comes from the smoothing stone. *Top:* the roughed surface. *Right:* the polished surface. The differences among them are readily apparent.

Corners, as usual, are difficult to do on the wheel. You have to maneuver the glass so that you get the maximum pressure. It can be awkward with small pieces. Don't apply so much pressure that you lose control. The speed of your movement back and forth across the wheel is not critical. Of course, be careful that in pressing and polishing you don't go too far and come out with a soft bevel.

A word about jeweler's rouge: Some workers prefer it to cerium oxide, but we hate it. If you want to try it, use it in a room that needs to be repainted. It makes a real mess.

The Shapes So Far

The three shapes we started with—the square, the star, and the shield—should now be given their final polishing. Since the felt wheel, like the cork, creates no facets, the only possible difficulty you can run into is rounding the bevels. Be especially careful with the outside curves of the shield where the mitred angles meet the top straight line or inside curve, whichever you have designed. Too long a polishing here can soften these mitres. The inside curves should be done on the dressed sides of the polishing wheels. Since you can't watch the felt wheel in action to any extent, polishing your first inside curve in the blind can be an experience. But it is fun, and you will soon get the feel of it.

Once your pieces are high-polished, take a good look at them. You have literally made something from nothing—an alchemy made possible by that fairy godmother the beveling machine.

CHAPTER 9

Interlude: A Clinic on Polishing and General Technique

Q: Are there different fiber wheels available for polishing with small bevelers?

A: We have worked with two types of fiber wheels. One was an aluminum-oxide fiber wheel, which we did not care for. The second, which we like very much, is a nylon fiber wheel embedded with a fine grit of silicon carbide rather than aluminum oxide. This composition leaves a smoother surface, allowing the wheel to do its job in slightly less time.

Q: Why does my fiber wheel scratch the glass?

A: Two things can cause scratching: (1) A new fiber wheel should be initially dressed to remove the coarse surface fibers that will scratch. To do this, use the sawed rough end of a piece of hardwood and run it back and forth across your wheel to "soften" the fiber. (2) A dry fiber wheel will scratch the glass. Make sure that your wheel is thoroughly soaked with water initially, and rewet the wheel when it begins to turn a lighter brown.

Q: How much pressure should I use on the fiber wheel?

A: A good rule of thumb is to use as much pressure as you feel comfortable with. The more pressure you use, the faster you will achieve your desired surface. However, you will risk catching the edge of your glass on the upturn of the wheel. Also, too much pressure can cause the glass to sink into the wheel, allowing it to work on your mitre and thus softening the beveled edge. After several hours' practice, you will find that you will be able to use quite a bit of pressure without causing a softening or losing control of the piece. You will develop a hand sense for the angle of your bevel.

Q: I can't tell where the fiber wheel is working. Is there a bubble to look for?

A: Unlike the stone wheel, it is rather difficult to see your cutting

Fig. 9-1 A fiber wheel. These wheels take from five to ten hours to work in. The time thus spent, however, is well worthwhile.

surface with the fiber wheel. This wheel requires more of a feel rather than a visual technique. Make sure to hold your bevel on this wheel at the same angle as you did on the piece from the roughing stage, and move it in the same manner. This will assure that you are polishing only your beveled surface (Fig. 9-2).

Q: The fiber wheel leaves deep striations in the bevel. Am I doing something wrong?

A: Yes and no. This wheel, by the nature of its composition, will leave some lines or striations in the glass very similar to the pumice lines left by the cork wheel. The more time you spend on this step, the deeper and more obvious these lines will become. To relieve this problem, spend more time on your stone wheel removing as many facets as possible instead of relying too heavily on the fiber wheel. This will shorten the time the fiber wheel needs to give you the desired surface.

Q: Can the fiber wheel cause facets? I seem to notice more now than I did when I left the stone wheel.

A: If you hold your glass in one spot long enough on any wheel, a low spot or facet will occur. However, this shouldn't happen if you move the piece constantly. The reason why you think there are more facets now than when you left the stone is because the fiber wheel is removing the deep haze left from the stone wheel. This makes the facets more visible. The fiber wheel removes only the deepest haze, however; the surface will still be hazy. This comes off with the felt.

Q: Can I use the edge of my 10″ fiber to polish tight inside curves instead of using a smaller wheel?

A: Unlike the felt wheel, the fiber edge cuts much too roughly and would ridge the glass. Use the 7″ or 4″ fiber wheel surface.

Q: If my fiber wheel bounces back and forth, what should I look for?

A: On the 10″ fiber, check to make sure that the flanges are tightly secured inside the fiber ring. If this should happen with the 7″ or 4″ wheels, check your bushings and locking flange (see Fig. 4-22).

Q: What exactly is the fiber wheel supposed to do? I have a difficult time seeing any difference between the surface left from the stone wheel and that left from the fiber wheel.

A: The purpose of the fiber is to semipolish and remove facets. The surface of your bevel will still be hazy from the stone, but it will be more uniform and smoother. To understand what the fiber does, rough out a piece of glass on your diamond wheel. Then smooth it on your stone wheel, skip the fiber wheel, and polish it on the felt. This rough, wiggly surface that is left is what your fiber wheel is removing and making smooth.

Q: My felt wheel tends to wobble. Why?

A: The density of the felt throughout the wheel may vary. Also the arbor hole could be slightly off center. When buying a felt wheel, try to get one that has felt uniformly built around a 1″ bushing. If the density of the felt is the same throughout, you will have a truer-running wheel. You can still polish with a slight wobble, however. Fortunately, polishing with the felt wheel is the simplest of the beveling steps. Maybe that is why many of these wheels do wobble.

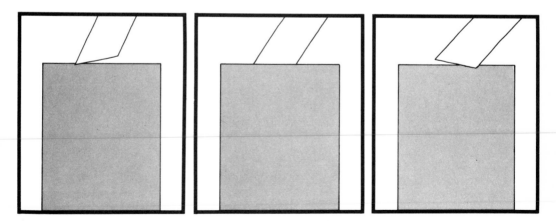

Fig. 9-2 The bevel must be held on the fiber wheel at the same angle as on the roughing wheel. The diagram in the *center* is correct; angles shown at left and right are common errors.

Q: My felt wheel dries out so quickly that it seems I'm always applying the cerium oxide mixture.

A: About five minutes before using your wheel, wet it with the cerium oxide mixture while your machine is turned off. Then, right before use, rewet the wheel. Your wheel will soak up a good amount of the mixture and throw off any excess. After this has been done, the mixture can be reapplied while the machine is running.

It is also possible that you are mixing the cerium oxide and water too thick, which will cause it to cake and be thrown off the wheel. The mixture should be similar in consistency to latex paint. You could apply it with a paintbrush. Remember to rough up your nap with a brush from time to time, however. Another tip on wetting your wheel is to dip a scrub brush into the cerium oxide mixture and apply it to the wheel while it is turning. This lifts up the nap of the felt. If, after several hours' use, a thick buildup of cerium oxide accumulates on the surface of the wheel, remove it by holding the edge of a piece of glass to the wheel until the felt is again exposed (see Fig. 8-4).

Q: How do I polish a very tight inside curve on such a large wheel?

A: The edge of the wheel is used for tight inside curves. For a larger polishing surface, round one edge of your wheel by dressing it as described or with 100-grit sandpaper. A right-handed person will usually dress the left edge of the wheel, and a left-handed person will dress the right edge.

Q: What happens if I make my felt wheel too wet?

A: If you do this and then turn off the machine, all the water sinks to the bottom of the wheel. When you turn the machine on again, it will bounce badly from the uneven balance of this wheel. The only way to rectify the now-lopsided wheel is to let it dry out completely. This takes several hours. You should wet the felt with the cerium oxide mixture only to a depth of $\frac{1}{4}''$. If you wet it to $\frac{1}{2}''$, you will have a problem.

Q: What technique on the felt wheel will help remove the surface left from the fiber wheel?

A: Cross-wheel polishing, as shown in Fig. 9-3, and permitting your glass to develop the necessary wet-heat friction against the wheel.

Q: Couldn't pumice be used in place of cerium oxide on the felt wheel for polishing? It's cheaper.

A: Yes, we've tried it. Using the finest pumice available, we achieved a polished surface. However, not with the same brilliance that results with using cerium oxide. It is all up to personal preference whether you trade quality for cost.

Q: Do you have any other suggestions to help keep the felt wheel from drying out so fast?

A: This is a very popular question. Here are a few new suggestions: (1) Keep a wet sponge under your wheel, but remember to remove it when not using the machine. The wheel will pick up too much water in the one spot and warp and swell. (2) Hold a hacksaw horizontally across the face of the felt, as with the cork wheel, to groove the material. This gives the cerium oxide mixture more of a surface to adhere to.

Q: What do I do if I soften a mitre accidentally?

A: Go back to the stone to resharpen it. You need not go all the way back to the diamond. A light touch on the stone won't take off very much glass, whereas the diamond may take off too much.

Q: What about a diamond disk for horizontal roughing instead of the vertical diamond wheel?

A: Nothing grinds better than a diamond, but the disk would be very expensive just because of the surface area you want exposed.

Q: What about vertical Carborundum wheels. Are they useful?

A: Some of the old-time bevelers worked on the side of their cast-iron wheel for inside curves, or they had vertical Carborundum wheels before vertical diamonds came into use. Carborundum wheels are still around, but we don't use them much today. They make a rougher cut than the diamond, and you can't work on them nearly so fast or cleanly. Carborundum wheels, while cheaper than diamond wheels, wear out faster. They also lose their shape and are harder to dress. Our experience with them has not been that favorable.

Q: How can I tell if my mitres are softening on the cork wheel?

A: The initial indicator of softening bevels is the slight haze that begins to appear on the surface of the glass. This would be the flat surface directly adjacent to the angle.

Q: Can I do a straight-line bevel on the vertical wheel?

A: Yes, certainly. You do a small area at a time as opposed to roughing the entire surface on the horizontal wheel. Never go

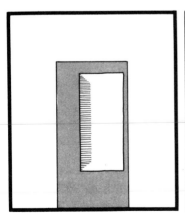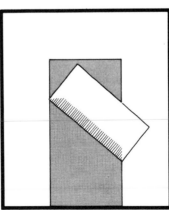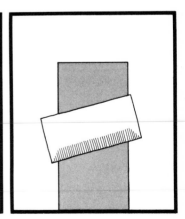

Fig. 9-3 Cross-wheel polishing on the felt wheel will help remove any surface striations left by the fiber wheel.

with the shape of the vertical wheel or you will get an uneven bevel. You can work the vertical wheel diagonally, coming across the diamond, but if you tip the glass just slightly, you risk catching the end of the glass in the wheel.

Q: Is there a difference between the larger commercial bevelers and the studio models?

A: The main difference is in size, although there are some design differences. The principles, though, are exactly the same. The horizontal wheels for the larger machines have a well in the center of the wheel. This contains the water reservoir in the sandstone wheel and the slurry in the cast-iron wheel.

Q: I have a lot of trouble with the stone wheel. How can I spend less time at it?

A: One way might be to do some of your smoothing on the cast-iron wheel. As you complete the roughing, you might cut the amount of slurry drip and increase the proportion of water. Or use a finer grit. This would partly smooth the roughed surface, giving the stone less work to do and thus cutting down on the amount of time you spend at it.

PART II: Design

CHAPTER 10
Pencil Bevels and Other Designed Shapes

The results that can be achieved in designing with bevels run the gamut from overwhelming to novel to bizarre to confusing, but rarely will the viewer stand completely passive in front of a beveled design. The effects are cumulative; that is to say, they are anchored in the crafting of the individual unit, as in any pieced design. Bevels differ from stained-glass pieces in that they contribute dimension, reflection, and the prism effects that are unique to them alone. A multiplicity of shapes is possible, not only the geometric ones in Part I—the square, shield, circle, and star—but asymmetrical designs that are limited only by the imagination. These shapes can be enhanced by "brilliant work"—notching, beading, zipper cutting, honeycombing, engraving—so that each shape has within itself permutations that modify its effect on its neighbors, whether the neighbors are other bevels or pieces of stained glass.

With so many possibilities in easy reach, it is no wonder that a craftsperson in glass latches onto bevels in order to make an artistic statement. In Chapter 12 several artists will do just this. We will see beveled works that transcend the overdone Victorian approach. We will see fascinating glass elements that are given new scope to express their own personality and to compliment and enhance stained glass. One of the starting points in such a design is the pencil bevel.

The Pencil Bevel

The pencil bevel is so called because it is narrow and is mitred like the side of a pencil. Many shapes other than the popular S can be pencil beveled; straight lines and single curves do very nicely. As we have previously mentioned, in a pencil bevel there is no untouched glass surface; the entire piece has been beveled. The top surface has been reduced to a ridge running (usually) the length of the bevel with two mitred ends.

The S shape is composed, reasonably enough, of two inside and two outside curves. Usually the inside curves are done on

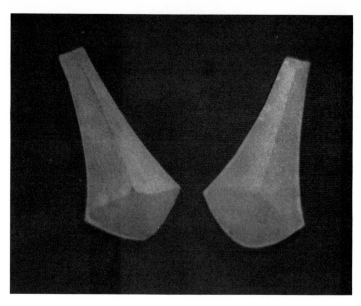

Fig. 10-1 Teardrop pencil bevels in the rough.

the diamond wheel, and the outside curves are done on the horizontal wheels. Of course you can do the entire shape on the diamond following the instructions in Chapter 4. However, because here the curves are "back to back," there are some things to watch out for. If you start with one of the inside curves, rough the entire curve, but try to come slightly under the halfway point to that central mitre. Do the same thing when roughing the corresponding outside curve. This leaves a small flat spot along the central ridge. The reason for doing this is that in creating the thin margin completely in the rough you may find parts of the edge beginning to chip. This can be very difficult to fix. But if you leave some space, say $\frac{1}{16}''$, you can let the entire mitre grow into it from both sides and there will be no chipping. We leave more room when roughing the outside curve than the inside one simply because this curve is harder to accomplish and can creep up to the edge more slyly. The stone can take care of even a $\frac{1}{8}''$ flat surface.

A few hints on technique: If you happen to go over the margin of this central mitre—just the opposite of what we advise above— you have to push the line back from the other side. Every time you do this, you remove more glass and the angle starts to diminish. Therefore, you can't do this too often. It is best, if you do overshoot the margin, to start over on a new piece.

We complete each curve in the rough before starting the next. First we rough the upper inner curve and the lower one; then we do the same with the two outer curves. Rough both curves before going on to the stone.

The S shape can be difficult to handle the first time out. The trick is to concentrate on one curve at a time, even if you have to split that curve into two different portions. You must be careful that you don't concentrate so much that you begin to get two different facets. Of course, a full sweep is difficult and awkward to watch as you go. You have to keep an eye on all the factors, such as where the glass is touching the wheel, where your hands are, and whether the bevel is going off the edge of the wheel. This is all compounded by the fact that you are dealing with a very slim piece of glass to begin with. Nevertheless, you must be able to see what you are doing, so don't hunch up and don't get tense. Do try to position yourself so that you don't get in your own way. Practice this double inside-curve sweep until you thoroughly understand the technique; then go to the outside curve.

S-shape pencil bevels are usually mitred on the ends as well as down the center. These end mitres meet the central ridge at distances that are determined by your design. However, there are certain guidelines to follow. In general, if the pencil bevel is 1″ wide, the mitre is $\frac{1}{2}$″ wide—half the width of the piece of glass if you want it even on both sides. Usually, then, the mitred ends would be also that measurement, following the width of one of the side mitres.

Pencil bevels are often used in lettering, and this is good exercise in this type of bevel. You don't want to spell "finis" to your career, though, so don't get totally absorbed in lettering at the beginning. But if you want to do some lettering, keep those mitred ends in mind. You might want to make them extra steep here. Make them

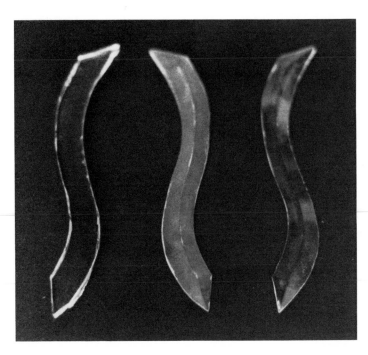

Fig. 10-2 The S shape. *Left:* the glass blank. *Middle:* the roughed pencil bevel. *Right:* the polished end result.

Fig. 10-3 Polishing the pencil bevel at the fourth station.

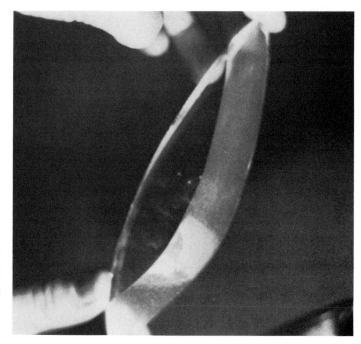

Fig. 10-4 The feather shape. One edge of the shape has been roughed. Since this is to be a pencil bevel, you would rough the other side to match this one in depth, leaving only a ridge of glass between the two surfaces.

as narrow and steep as possible, rather than long and gradual, so as not to throw the lettering off. The reason for these end mitres, other than design, is to be able to get the ends into the lead or zinc channel. You can make up your own dimensions for the mitres, but they at least should all match one another if you intend to use them in a regular pattern.

In a window, long mitres at the end of pencil bevels can appear to be a poor design concept. They tend to make the bevels look flat at the ends and steep in width. This is an optical illusion that you may find disappointing after all the work you have put into the piece.

It is also fun to work with irregularly shaped pencil bevels. If the piece of glass you are pencil beveling is itself irregular—say you have a piece of glass $\frac{1}{2}''$ wide that tapers up to $1''$—the discrepancy will affect the mitred ends. You might want to make the thinner end mitre steeper than the other side. Our usual approach to any of these asymmetrical shapes is to think halfway about the bevel—halfway across and halfway down. It's a nice design trick.

Rough Designs

Another design "trick"—and it is really more than that—is to leave some surfaces of your bevels unsmoothed and unpolished, just as they come off the diamond or cast-iron wheel. This ground-glass effect can add a startling note of texture. With high polished surfaces all around, this single element can add emphasis where it may be most needed. Of course, any good effect can be overdone and confuse the eye rather than be pleasing to it. But it is important to remember that just because the beveling process follows successive steps on the wheels, your artistic impulses need not be enslaved to the machine. You are the one in control, not the beveling machine, regardless of how sophisticated it may be.

In addition to the different textures that are available to you in a roughed surface, degrees of roughing can provide subtle distinctions even in a cluster of rough bevels, so you can get shadowing as well. Sometimes you can part rough and part high-polish a single surface. This is yet another point of design grammar within the language of beveled artistry. In fact, anything goes, if it adds up to the effect that you intended. Effect for its own sake, however, soon becomes boring.

Making Jewels

One dramatic way to make a jewel is to take a piece of $\frac{1}{4}''$ plate outside and support it vertically. Then with a BB gun (or a slingshot using BB shot), shoot at the glass. An interesting cone-shaped jewel will pop out the other side. The fracturing of the front of the glass by the shot sets up strain lines along a triangular pathway through the surface. It doesn't seem to matter how close to or how far away you are from the glass. But it is important that the glass be perfectly vertical. You can get different size jewels depending on the size of the shot. If the glass is slanted, however, either the jewel won't pop out of the glass or you will have a jewel

A
Series
of
Designed
Samples

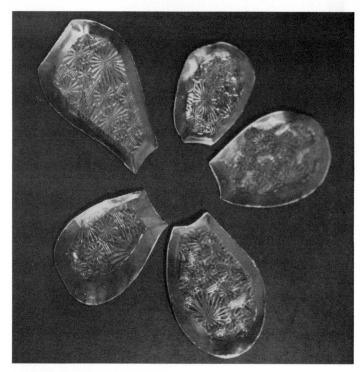

Fig. 10-5A Beveled flower petals. We used some old glass that had already been stamped with a pattern. You can find interesting old glass scrap in junkyards and in the scrap bins of local glaziers.

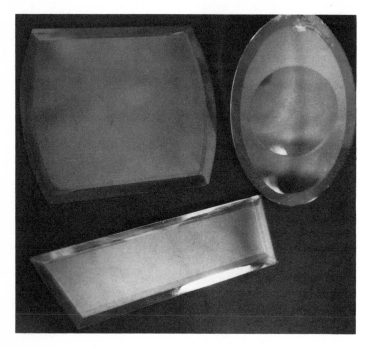

Fig. 10-5B Completed beveled pieces of various shapes. The oval on the right has an additional advantage in its central circle, which has been ground into the glass and polished to perfection. (Courtesy Nervo International Suppliers.)

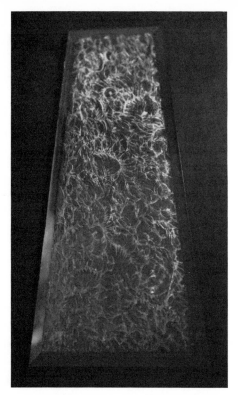

Fig. 10-5C A glue-chipped, beveled lamp panel. (Courtesy Cherry Creek Enterprise, Denver.)

Fig. 10-5D A beveled lamp panel. The glass was first glue chipped. Note the engraved lines within. (Courtesy Cherry Creek Enterprise, Denver.)

Fig. 10-5E A lamp panel, engraved on a beveling machine. The sanded surface effect was achieved not by sandblasting, but by holding the glass flat for a brief period on the cast-iron wheel with 100 grit. This gives an even sandblasted finish.

Fig. 10-5F A bevy of bevels.

Fig. 10-5G Cartoon for beveled glass with some of the glass pieces overlaid. (Courtesy Harry Bullock and Linda Neely, PRISM Glass.)

Fig. 10-5*H* A beveled sunrise. (Courtesy Harry Bullock and Linda Neely, PRISM Glass.)

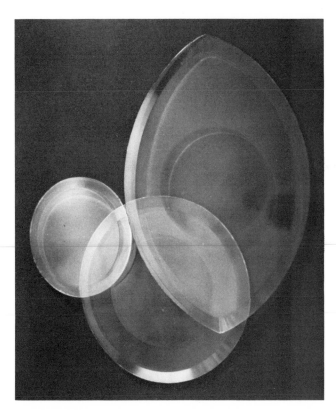

Fig. 10-5*I* Wheels within wheels. A cluster of beveled circles and ovals. (Courtesy Nervo International.)

Fig. 10-5J A typical glue-chipped beveled window. Repaired by Harry Bullock and Linda Neely.

Fig. 10-5K A typical Victorian beveled window. (Designed and owned by Steve Williams; made by Harry Bullock.)

Fig. 10-5L A design employing multiple copper-foiled small-piece bevels. (Courtesy Harry Bullock and Linda Neely, PRISM Glass.)

Fig. 10-5M A circular beveled window. (Courtesy Harry Bullock.)

Fig. 10-5N Two roughed squares. At bottom is an example of a multibeveled square surface.

Fig. 10-6 Colored glass made into jewels by beveling. At bottom right: a cone shape from clear plate.

with irregular edges. You can grind these down on the machine, which is kind of fun. Whenever you make jewels this way, wear safety glasses and watch out for ricocheting of the BB.

If you prefer to make jewels in a less frivolous way, you can make them in great variety on the beveling machine. Just pick a shape and go to it. We like to use chunk glass (dalle pieces), since it is colored and comes in interesting asymmetrical shapes that can be further modified on the beveling machine. Clear plate glass $\frac{1}{2}''$ or even $\frac{3}{8}''$ also produces a variety of symmetrical shapes to suit your needs, whether round, oval, cone shaped, square, triangular, or rectangular. Glue-chipped glass will provide an interesting textured surface for many jewels. If you want colored pieces, several

Fig. 10-7 Roughing a jewel. When working with small pieces, try to keep your fingers off the wheel to prevent abrasions.

Fig. 10-8 A completed glass jewel in a smooth cone shape.

companies (see Sources of Supply) are starting to produce colored plate glass for the beveling hobbyist. There isn't much to be had yet, but the supply should increase in the future.

Producing jewels is not a special art in itself. All you have to do to make distinctive ones is to add your own creative personality

Fig. 10-9 Colored bevels produced from thick pieces of stained glass made specifically for beveling. (Courtesy Steven R. Johnson.)

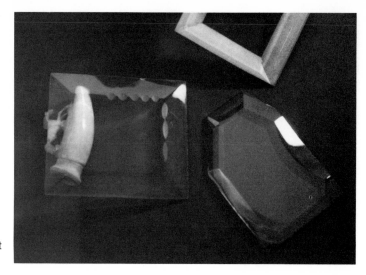

Fig. 10-10 Bevels with different embellishments.

to the techniques discussed in Part I. For instance, creating a cone jewel is much the same as doing a beveled circle—except that with a jewel you are carrying the bevel over the entire surface of the glass. Do small sections, as you would a circle or an outside curve: That is, stop and turn and stop and turn until you close the circle. The result will be a conical shape. The best width glass to use is $\frac{3}{8}''$ and up; $\frac{1}{4}''$ plate, other than for the BB technique, is too thin for jewels.

Step Beveling

Step beveling can enhance a design, or it can exist as a design element in itself. As the name suggests, the glass presents a series of beveled surfaces that descend in a pattern of steps. Light reflects

Fig. 10-11 Some three-dimensional jewel-like forms. *Left:* a hand-blown sculpture, faceted and polished on the beveling machine. *Middle:* a glass pressed cube. *Right:* a heavy glass chunk faceted into a crystal. (Courtesy Linda Neely.)

Fig. 10-12 An amorphous piece of chunk glass, which can be faceted into interesting, beautiful objects if there are no air bubbles in the center. Bubbles will cause the piece to shatter.

differently from each step. On mirrors especially, you can get very interesting effects with step bevels.

To make a step bevel with one or more steps requires a fairly thick piece of plate glass; $\frac{3}{8}''$ will do, but $\frac{1}{2}''$ is better. The process of making a step bevel is:

1. Mark the ultimate width of your bevel on the glass. This will be the extreme slope of the angle. The basic angle will be a gradual one with a thick edge of glass left.
2. Rough out the sloping angle, but remember to leave the edge as thick as possible.
3. Divide the angle into one or more steps. If you want a single step, divide the angle in half. If you want two steps, divide the angle accordingly. Usually three steps is the most that can be beveled. Each step of course becomes narrower as others are added.
4. Make the second bevel. The slope of this angle will be less than the first.
5. Make the third bevel (if you have planned for one). This angle will be steeper than the second.
6. Rough all the steps, then smooth and polish them.

Another way to proceed in step beveling is to smooth and polish each step as you go. However, then you have to re-rough part of what you have just smoothed for the next bevel. We feel this method is not worth the effort.

Step Beveling

Fig. 10-13 *Step 1:* Make a wider bevel along the edge to be step beveled than along the other sides.

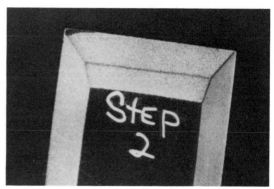

Fig. 10-14 *Step 2:* Angling the original bevel some distance from the beveled edge. This provides two separate angles.

Fig. 10-15 *Step 3:* Three angles can be made in the same manner, so long as you don't run out of room and you can keep the mitres even in width.

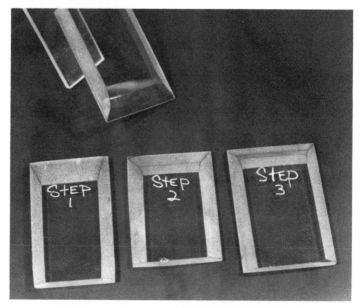

Fig. 10-16 The three steps in a step bevel. At top is the finished bevel.

Glass is almost the perfect illusionist, just as mirror is the perfect one. There are many optical effects possible with beveled glass, especially when you combine straight and curved lines and use both sides of the glass. In this way you are allowing the refractive power of the glass to heighten the illusion.

One of the many interesting features you can create is the bent-glass illusion. Cut a circle out of a thick piece of glass. Make a straight bevel on two sides of it on the cast-iron (or diamond) wheel. Next, turn the circle over. Between the two side bevels, make another straight bevel. Now when you look through the glass, it appears to be bent. You can also make a plaid effect, beveling back and forth on the two sides of the glass to produce interesting distortions. The bent-glass illusion is not only fun, but it gives you a lot of good beveling practice.

To curve a straight bevel in any area, place your straight-edge piece against the vertical diamond (or against the stone if you don't need too deep a curve) and hold it in one spot. The wheel will automatically scallop out the center of the bevel, thus curving it. The curve can be extended by moving the glass slightly to either side. You have to be careful when you do this that you don't scallop out too much. As is always the case, practice helps.

There are two ways to bevel mirror. The first is to bevel it before it is silvered, in which case the technique is the same as for beveling any plate glass. The second is to bevel it as mirror itself. The first process is the easier of the two, except then you are faced with the task of silvering the glass into mirror. We have found that silvering is best left to the experts in the field, since the process can be extremely tedious and time-consuming. It is hardly within the reach of most glass professionals, let alone the hobbyist, considering the equipment and chemicals—as well as the experience—that are needed to do a good job.

The latter technique, that of beveling mirror itself, is called blind beveling. The term gives some inkling as to its frustrations. Not only does it imply that you cannot see what you are doing—remember you are beveling with the mirror surface down, the backing up—but it is also difficult to prevent scratching the mirror during the procedure. Nevertheless, blind beveling can become, if not a way of life, at least an important ancillary process to your regular beveling. After a while you will develop a feel for the angle, and your hand sense will act as a guide. With a great deal of practice, you won't need your eyes at all. However, practice on scrap, since you will waste a lot of mirror before you perfect your technique. The more beveling you do before you tackle mirror, the easier mirror will be, since your hand sense will already be fairly sophisticated.

The plate must be kept scratch-free while you are working if it is going to be silvered for mirror, which will magnify every little

Optical Illusions

Curving Bevels

Beveling Mirror

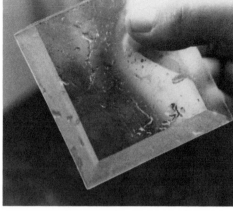

Fig. 10-17 Beveling a square. Three sides have been roughed. Note the evenness of the beveled edges.

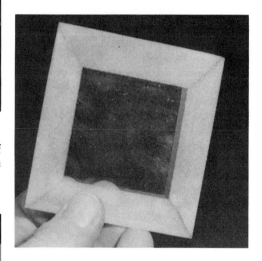

Fig. 10-18 Beveling both sides of a square. The back side has been left rough.

Fig. 10-19 The three-dimensional square: The glass has been beveled on both sides, the back side left rough, the front side polished. Note the effect of the polished surface. The polished mitre is $\frac{3}{8}''$ wide; the back rough one is $\frac{5}{8}''$ wide.

Fig. 10-20 The three-dimensional bevel seen from the polished surface.

158

Fig. 10-21 Roughing: Blind-beveling mirror stock. This is not an easy procedure even with small pieces. (Courtesy The Glass Bevel.)

scratch. One way to handle this problem is to tape the entire surface of the plate except for the area where you are working. Contact paper works well for this. Keep at least an inch away from the working end of the plate. If you are beveling mirror (blind beveling), you can tape the entire back surface to protect the silvering during the beveling process. The scratching is most likely to occur during the roughing process; one piece of silicon carbide can get on the silvered surface and scratch it badly when you wipe the back. Then you must have the whole thing re-silvered. It's better to tape it up.

Buying Bevels for Design Purposes

There is nothing wrong with buying bevels. You can even buy clusters of them and lead them up as part of your stained-glass panel. Or you could use them in a decorative piece. A number of companies sell bevels already made. The advantage of buying

Fig. 10-22 Roughing: A 1″ bevel in the making. This is the best way to do mirrors. First bevel the glass clear, then silver it or have it silvered. (Courtesy The Glass Bevel.)

Fig. 10-23 Playing with mirror. The oval and the long strip have been beveled. The long strip has had part of its mastic removed for effect.

bevels rather than making them is that you save time. However, purchasing items designed by somebody else is hardly a craft and certainly not an art. Of course, you can't make everything; otherwise you would be supplying your own flux and copper foil and lead.

The true craftsperson usually wants to create every designed item in the finished product. At the same time, he or she may be understandably shy about making the dollar commitment to a new craft, such as beveling. Interestingly enough, most of the people we have met who began working with bevels by buying them ready-made now own beveling machines and are making their own bevels. No doubt some of the bevels they first turn out are inferior to the commercial product, but at least they are their own. In the end that is what outweighs the time saved by purchasing someone else's bevels. So the more companies that sell bevel clusters to hobbyists, the better. We wish them luck. They are the purveyors of temptation. Sooner or later, after you have been introduced to commercial bevels, you will want to make them yourself. After all, that is what the hobby and crafts field is all about.

CHAPTER 11

Brilliant Work and Engraving

A thin (beveled) line exists between brilliant work and glass engraving. In fact, it is hard to tell where one technique leaves off and the other begins. We distinguish the two this way. Brilliant work encompasses certain surface modifications that enhance the play of light on a piece of beveled glass and give it additional sparkle or texture. Engraving is the actual cutting of a design into the glass surface in order to use the glass as an airy canvas. It has nothing to do with enhancing the play of light. You may not agree with these definitions, but they at least give us a starting point.

The Wheels

Four wheels are used for both brilliant work and glass engraving: two stone wheels and two felt wheels. Of course, you may use many more wheels, especially if you are going to get fairly involved in engraving. We limit our engraving technique mainly to what can be done on a beveling machine, not on an engraver. The wheels therefore are matched in pairs—one felt and one stone, both of which are dressed similarly.

Dressing the Wheels

Start out with a pair of 6″ by $\frac{1}{2}$″ stone wheels and a pair of felt wheels of the same dimension. One pair of wheels will be rounded; the other pair will be pointed to achieve different effects. The felts should be rounded or pointed as closely as possible to their corresponding stone wheels. The reason why you need two pairs is so that you don't have to keep redressing a single pair of stone and felt wheels. If you want a rounded stone today and a pointed one tomorrow, you will waste time redressing them. In addition, they will get smaller and smaller as you remove their surfaces to match the new shape. There is no need to have a cork wheel as an intermediate step in engraving. Since you will be grinding and polishing such a small surface area, you can go right from the stone wheel to the felt wheel without any problem.
Rounding your stone should take less than five minutes. To

Fig. 11-1 Two engraving stones and the felt wheels that go with them. The stones and the felt wheels must be shaped, either rounded or pointed depending on the effect you want to achieve.

point it, however, takes a good twenty to thirty minutes, since you will be removing quite a bit more stone than in rounding. We like to use an aluminum oxide stone because it is very dense and doesn't wear down readily even with the Carborundum dressing stick.

If you dress your stone wheels dry, wear a mask to protect your

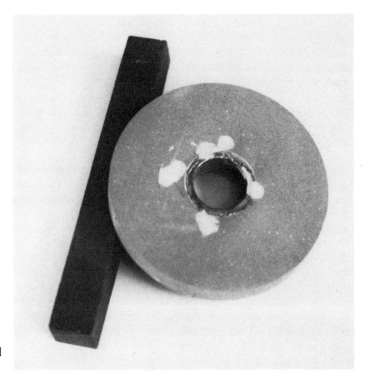

Fig. 11-2 An engraving wheel and a dressing stick for shaping it.

lungs from debris in the air. Dressing the stones wet is much safer, but grindings will gum up the wheel and dressing stick, so the process will take longer.

To round the stone, apply the dressing stick first to each rim corner and gradually dull their sharp outlines. Once these are dulled, roll the stick until you begin to get a rounded shape that looks workable. Apply as much pressure as you can without tiring your arm.

To dress the stone to a point, begin as though you were rounding it. Then angle the dressing stick at each side of the stone at an upward slant until the point of the stone starts to grow right in the center. What you want on your pointed wheel is exactly that— a nice sharp point. If you don't have it, you will find it difficult to keep the glass from sliding all over the wheel. A sharp point digs right into the glass; a dull one has trouble getting a bite, and the glass will show these hesitating attempts. Naturally, as you continue to use this point or edge, it begins to flatten. Eventually it will flatten so much that it will need to be redressed. This deformation doesn't occur with the rounded wheel, which, you will find, rarely needs to be redressed, if at all.

The Wheel Technique

Before you use the engraving wheels, you should check to see that the wheels are spinning as smoothly as possible. The worst thing that can happen is to have a bounce in a wheel as you are attempting to keep it firm against the glass surface. Watch the wheel for a minute or two before using it to see that the spin is steady. If the wheel bounces out of true, it would be best to dress a new stone, because the old one isn't going to contact the glass properly. Before you do this with a bouncing wheel, however, move it off the threads of the axle toward the smooth part of the shaft. This may help a lot. On the other hand, it may not. Whatever it takes, make sure that you have a smooth-running wheel. Otherwise you simply cannot engrave. You must have control.

Although you may want to wear a mask throughout the engraving process, we usually do not. We keep our stones wet with a moist sponge placed beneath them. This not only provides the moisture they need without having to spray them with the spigot— which tends to get everything wet—but it also prevents glass and stone dust from flying around.

To start engraving, press your glass slowly but firmly onto the turning wheel and allow the wheel to get a good bite into it before you move it around. This is true for both the sharp stone and the rounded one. If you try to move the glass before the wheel has effectively taken hold, it will skid, and few things look worse than these blurry marks on the glass. In the beginning you will get them, of course, and there's nothing you can do about them once they are there except to use the glass as a practice piece.

Once the stone has gotten a good bite into the glass, you can

Fig. 11-3 Dressing an engraving wheel.

slowly guide the glass along the path you want it to take. Use the pointed stone for anything that needs a deep wedge cut; use the rounded one for an oval shape. To polish these cuts, use the corresponding felts. Many workers simply do not bother to polish their engraving or brilliant work. Since these minibevels are so fine, you can polish or not depending on the extra effort you want to expend for the extra amount of effect.

We use our rounded stone for notching on bevels, honeycombing, and flower petals, which brings us to some of the terminology of brilliant work.

Fig. 11-4 Engraving wheels set up on the Studio Model beveler. The wheel on the left is rounded; the wheel on the right is pointed. The wet sponges beneath provide enough water to keep the stones properly moist.

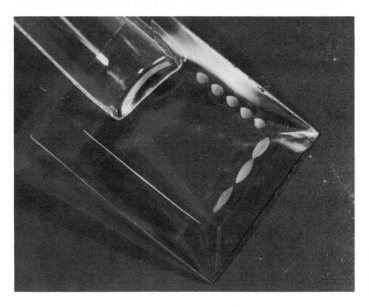

Fig. 11-5A Notchings on a beveled edge, done with an engraving wheel.

Notching can be done with the pointed or the rounded wheel simply by pressing the glass briefly against the wheel. The shape of the notch depends on which surface you use and how long and how much pressure you apply to the glass. Notching is usually done on the polished bevel, and it appears as a sort of slice when the pointed wheel is used. When the rounded wheel is used, the shape of the notches is oval and is called beading.

An Ensemble of Brilliant Work

Notching

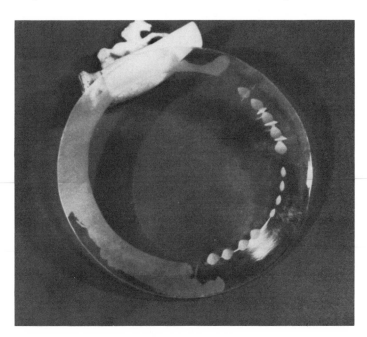

Fig. 11-5B Other examples of notching. Many shapes can be done for effect.

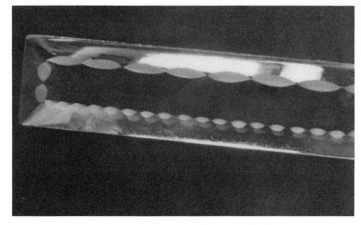

Fig. 11-6 Three examples of etching of a beveled margin—all done with the rounded stone.

Beading

A bead is the oval notch produced by the rounded wheel. It is not readily apparent as a single notch. Usually these shapes are done in multiples. Notching and beading can be intermixed in a piece.

Zipper Cutting

Zipper cutting is a string of notches done with the pointed wheel in a series of quick dashes. Each one still has a typical rhomboid shape. A string of them will look like one side of a zipper. Notches and zipper-cutting work are generally polished with a hard flint felt. Hard felt is specific for this work, since an ordinary felt will not maintain a pointed shape.

Honeycombing

Honeycombing is one of our favorite techniques. In honeycombing, usually the entire surface of the glass is used, as opposed to only the breakline in notching, beading, and zipper cutting. Use the rounded wheel and, starting in the center of the glass, make an entire row of little ovals. Then go below or above it to make another row. Make this row touch those to either side of the first row. This squares off the entire row. Stagger each row to the neighboring one like brickwork. This will give you the six-sided shape of a honeycomb. Each mark is then polished with the rounded felt wheel to keep the shape. You must polish each and every oval on the wheel.

Honeycombing is usually done on glass before it has been beveled. The reason for doing this is that if you bevel first, you may find it difficult to honeycomb the entire area around it, whereas you can always figure where the bevel will be and leave room for it when you honeycomb. Remember, you want to honeycomb the entire surface—there should be no bare areas—but you don't want to go into the mitre. It doesn't matter if you honeycomb into the beveled area before it is worked because you are going to be removing that glass anyway. But you don't want to go into that area once it has been beveled and disturb that mitre.

Engraving

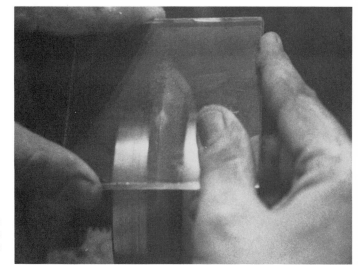

Fig. 11-7 Engraving a piece of plate using the pointed stone. The glass is just beginning to receive the stone edge.

Fig. 11-8 Engraving a piece of glass with a 4″ aluminum oxide stone that has been dressed to a pointed edge. The first step is to cross two straight lines in the center.

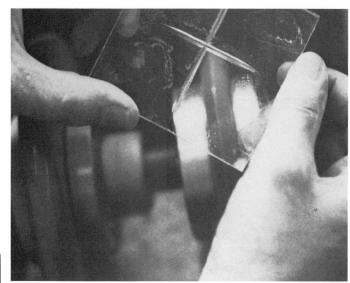

Fig. 11-9 The second step is to cross two diagonal lines within it. Even a simple project such as this takes on a life of its own in glass. We scalloped the upper edge of the square just to see the effect.

167

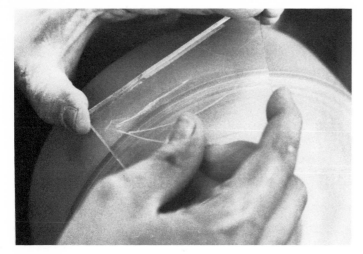

Fig. 11-10 Engraving with the edge of the vertical aluminum oxide stone. It takes practice to get good lines, since it is difficult to manipulate the edge against the glass. Also, the wheel is turning too fast for accurate control. With practice, however, you can come up with some adequate lines if you keep the project simple.

Fig. 11-11 Practice engraving marks with the engraving stone.

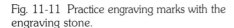

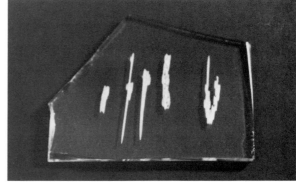

Fig. 11-12 A rough flower sketch engraved in a beveled circle.

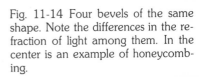
Fig. 11-14 Four bevels of the same shape. Note the differences in the refraction of light among them. In the center is an example of honeycombing.

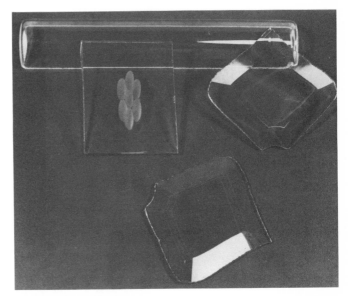

Fig. 11-13 A commercially engraved bevel. You can mix these with your own for effect. (Courtesy Cherry Creek Enterprise.)

Fig. 11-15 Examples of engraving.

Fig. 11-16 A sandblasted beveled piece. Note how the two effects enhance each other. (Courtesy Nervo International.)

Fig. 11-17 Engraved bevels. (Courtesy Cherry Creek Bevels and Jewels, Denver.)

Fig. 11-18 A dramatic engraved bevel done by hand with a stone wheel. (Courtesy Cherry Creek Enterprise.)

170

Although a certain amount of superficial engraving can be done with the stones we have described, we don't mean to imply that true artistic engraving can be turned out on your beveler. It isn't meant to be an engraving machine, and this chapter isn't meant to turn you into a wheel engraver. We merely want to introduce you to the subject through the beveling modalities of brilliant work.

Wheel Engraving

True wheel engraving is an art in itself and requires a different machine from your beveler. The speed of the motor is absolutely critical to an engraver. The machine needed would have a variable speed DC motor with very heavy torque. It also needs an extremely steady axle. It is possible to build an engraving machine if you keep these two principles in mind. We have seen homemade machines that do beautiful work in the hands of skilled operators. Some machines are little more than an axle driven by a motor with the appropriate wheels attached, the motor powering the axle via pulley systems. We have also seen magnificent work done by engravers using a hand wheel. But this is another subject altogether—and, actually, another book.

CHAPTER 12

Personally Speaking: Conversations with Beveling Artists

Allen H. Graef:
Colored Bevels

I was trained to be a potter, which is the same thing as being trained to be a starving artist. While working on my master's degree, I took a private class in stained glass because I knew that someday I would own a house and would want to use stained glass in it. Then at Alfred University, where I was teaching ceramics, I discovered some old beveling equipment. I started to experiment with it and got fascinated. The next thing I knew I was building my own. My knowledge of stained-glass seemed to dovetail with beveling. And, actually, glass and ceramics aren't all that far apart.

I think being a perfectionist is a good thing for a beveler. The discipline lends itself to this state of mind. I've always been a perfectionist, at least in certain things, and beveling is one of them. I confine all my grinding materials to their own niches so that they don't contaminate one another. I don't need silicon carbide in the cerium oxide. When I'm beveling, I confine the clutter to each station and wash up between steps. It keeps things pure.

Perhaps as part of my perfectionism I take pleasure in clean and shiny objects. I get a feeling of satisfaction after I have cleaned and waxed an automobile. I can stand back and look at it sparkle in the sunlight. It is almost like reaching the state of Satori, the experience of mind that Zen Buddhist monks seek to attain. This all has a part in my glass beveling.

I constantly think about expanding the medium: for instance, making thick bevels with the bevel meandering over the glass from maybe $\frac{1}{4}''$ to as much as $2''$ in some spots. I currently enjoy what thick colored beveled glass can do in an autonomous panel. It is from such experiments that I have developed new products for the stained-glass industry, such as thick glass in colors for beveling and thick-cast dimensional shapes that can be used in place of jewels. Colored bevels have their problems, like all stained glass.

First, of course, is the difficulty in finding colored plate. Second, colored glass reacts differently to the beveling procedure. Blues and greens tend to crack when polished, and they don't take the heat of the felt wheel well. But the result is worth the effort. Colored bevels have all the lushness of stained glass. In addition, each color absorbs its own spectrum of light as the light waves refract from the surface. They are like little selective filters. I think colored bevels add not only to the clear glass but also to the stained-glass elements that I use. And then there's that dimensional effect too.

Before I design a beveled window, I try to have as exact an idea as possible from my client as to subject matter. If the design is to be a symmetrical one, there is usually no problem. But with specific subject matter, I can spend many hours on artwork, unless I'm designing with a free rein. Then the artwork can take as little time as an hour. My designs are spontaneous and usually begin from some mood or feeling. About halfway through the design, I start thinking of bevels. So I place the remaining emphasis on beveled glass. When I think of bevels, I don't limit myself only to beveled glass; I consider different techniques, such as beveling both sides of the glass to get a more optical and dimensional quality. I decide on the thickness of glass I want to use. I also think of colored bevels whenever and wherever I can. After the design is worked out I proceed with the cut lines, which I draw on with a Sharpie marker. I then mark all the pieces to be beveled and start cutting.

I use an oil-feed cutter with a small pattern head for just about everything: plate glass, blown glass, rolled glass. I have a pair of metal running pliers handy for breaking and a $\frac{1}{2}''$ jaw Knipex pliers for small breaking and grozzing. I usually have something for taping the glass nearby. I rough-cut the glass for beveling, then seam up the edges with a 4" by $\frac{1}{2}''$ diamond wheel. This is the only diamond wheel I use. I place the pieces of glass in a wooden rack next to the roughing machine, within easy reach. Then I start beveling. When I bevel, I hand-hold the glass throughout.

I rough on a 28" diameter cast-iron horizontal wheel with a 120 finish and use 120-mesh silicon carbide as a grinding medium. I use 120 mesh for most jobs, but if I am beveling thick glass, I will use 80-mesh silicon carbide first and then 120 mesh. If I am producing a bevel of 1" or more, or a bevel 6' in length, I use 80 mesh first, then 120 mesh, and finally 400-mesh silicon carbide. By using these three mesh sizes on a wide bevel, I am able to produce a *most perfect* bevel.

I use 120 mesh and 400 mesh if I am blind-beveling mirror. If I am making a large mirror, I first bevel the plate glass and then silver it. During the roughing stage I keep a container of water right above the wheel and toward the back so that I can wash the glass and keep track of the depth of the bevel. If I am beveling a large piece of glass, I usually have a barrel of water close by for washing. I have a drain on the roughing machine that goes into a bucket so that I can reclaim the silicon carbide that washes into it. Since silicon carbide is an expensive raw material, I try to reclaim as much as possible.

I bevel my inside curves on the edge of the cast-iron wheel, which I have rounded just slightly. I find that I get a better bevel on this wheel than on a vertical diamond wheel. To keep everything organized, I rough all the pieces at one time. After the shapes have been roughed, I wash them and put them into racks next to the smoothing stone.

My smoothing stone is a 30″ diameter, 4″ thick sandstone quarried in England. A gentle flow of water is all that is necessary to smooth the glass. I have a drain on the machine to the main disposal line.

The smoothing stage is the most critical and tedious part of the whole beveling process. My stone is tapered just slightly with a rounded edge so that the water can flow off the bottom portion. I attach a sponge to one side of the machine against the side of the stone to remove the excess water. This prevents the water from splashing on me and around the work area. When I smooth a bevel, I use the entire stone surface. This wears the stone evenly and allows it to be trued rapidly.

Every now and then the stone becomes glazed: It looks polished when it is dry and feels smooth as glass to the touch. At that point it must be deglazed. I do this by first holding an 80-grit silicon carbide stone to the surface with the machine operating. Then I hold a 400-grit stone to the surface, making sure that I cover the whole smoothing stone surface. After this, I flood the stone with warm water. This removes all the loose gritty material from the stone. If this deglazing process is not done, the stone begins to "grab" the glass, and it can fling it across the room.

Once you have a stone that is finished just right, smoothing takes little time and you get a very nice surface. All straight bevels and outside curves are done on the smoothing stone. All inside curves are smoothed on a vertical 12″ diameter 200-grit silicon carbide wheel. I use a 4″ diameter wheel for tight inside curves. If I am smoothing a large piece with a wide bevel, I turn off all background light and work with a spotlight on the glass. This enables me to see more of the action of the stone on the glass.

Polishing is next, and it is done in two stages. The first polishing is done with pumice. I mix pumice and water to a slurry consistency and apply it to a 36″ diameter solid cork wheel. The wheel is 4″ thick and rotates vertically. I apply "F" grade pumice with a sponge at regular intervals. Sometimes I use "O" grade pumice first, then "F" grade to attain a better finish, particularly on wide bevels and when blind beveling.

About every two months or so, I true the cork wheel with a Sureform woodworking tool. This does the job very rapidly. I use the cork wheel for everything: for inside curves (which I do on the wheel edge), outside curves, and straight bevels.

I save all my used pumice and recycle it for cleaning leaded glass. Pumice is much better than plaster of paris or sawdust for cleaning windows. It scours the lead, absorbs the excess flux and putty, polishes the glass brilliantly, and doesn't create the mess and dust that plaster of paris and whiting do.

For the final polishing, I use a 24″ diameter vertical felt wheel. I apply a mixture of cerium oxide and water to the felt until it is saturated. I let it spin for a few minutes, apply cerium oxide in pressed stick form, and then apply more cerium oxide slurry. Now the wheel is ready for polishing. If I have prepared it properly, the wheel needs only an occasional wetting with more slurry or just water. If the wheel is allowed to dry out even slightly, the friction will heat the glass and cause cracking or burning. So wetting the wheel from time to time is a must. There is a treated cerium oxide on the market that is alright for large, linear beveling machines, but I find it unsatisfactory for the beveling that I do. It just doesn't polish to the brilliance that I want.

When the felt wheel is prepared properly, it will "cut" or polish the glass surface to an optical brilliance in just seconds. When the work is finished, I let the felt wheel spin dry. If you don't do this, the water in the felt will flow to the bottom of the wheel and leave a lump in the felt the next time it is used. If the wheel needs to be trued, I hold a piece of sharp $\frac{1}{4}$″ plate glass against the back of the wheel wedged against the mounting, with the wheel in motion. The lumps can be scraped out with this technique. Sometimes I use an old hacksaw blade for truing the felt wheel. I keep a container of water on a shelf at the front of the felt wheel for washing the glass. I also have a container for the cerium oxide on this shelf. At the end of the day, I toss out the water because the wet cerium oxide produces an unpleasant odor if left overnight. Another way to prevent this is to put a teaspoon of vinegar and a gallon of water in the container. But I prefer to throw the water out.

For glue-chipped bevels, I have another cerium oxide polishing station. I first bevel the glass that has already been chipped. All the beveling steps are the same except for polishing. I polish the chipped bevels on a horizontal wheel with a synthetic surface that holds the cerium oxide. In polishing the chipped bevel, I work toward the chipped area. This eliminates the lines in the bevel that glue chipping can produce. By using synthetics, the odor that can accompany cerium oxide is eliminated.

A word about window construction. I have started to construct beveled panels with as hard a lead as I can find. I prefer a lead with a high amount of tin and antimony. I then run bracing through the panel with $\frac{3}{8}$″ steel. I bend the brace bar so that it blends into the design and is hidden. Although I use lead for expediency, I still prefer to build a panel with zinc came. I put little cushions of lead against a bevel when I am leading up. These are made from $\frac{1}{4}$″ U-channel came. I find that even horseshoe nails can chip a bevel in the leading-up process. It's discouraging to have this happen right at the end to a piece that you've been so careful with through so many stages.

Some of my sources of supply are Cecil Wilson, H.C.H. Chemicals, for thick $\frac{7}{8}''$ dalle glass in many colors. I cut them up and then bevel them. Salem Distributors supplies silicon carbide and pumice. Sommer and Maca supplies glass machinery, as well as cerium oxide. I get the wheels for my beveler from Carborundum Corporation. As for $\frac{1}{4}''$ colored glass for beveling, my own company, The Glass Bevel, is currently in the process of manufacturing it. (Note: See Sources of Supply for addresses.)

Mark Bogenrief: Jeweled Windows

If it is possible to be addicted to an activity, I am addicted to beveling. Beveling, in fact, has produced a complete turnaround in my life. It all began with a strike at a packing plant, which left my wife and I without jobs. My father and brother had a small glass shop, and I went there to learn how to work in stained glass. I worked on repairs and commissions. My father, who is an antique dealer as well, had found a complete set of Henry Lange beveling equipment ten years earlier sitting in a farm yard for scrap. He bought it and stored it. One day, looking through a glass magazine, I saw an advertisement for a beveling school in Denver. I signed up for the beveling course, and when I returned, I set up the Lange equipment.

I continued to do beveling repairs, and we added beveling to our window designs in the shop. Soon we were doing large custom beveling jobs for other studios, and that literally got to be a grind. Then we were fortunate enough to buy some old, ornate Victorian windows. My wife and I started to repair them in a room in our house that we had fixed up as a studio. When we ran out of the old windows, we decided to fabricate our own decorative ones. We've been going strong ever since.

Here are some of the ways I run a piece through the beveling stages. For rough grinding I use 120-grit silicon carbide for outside curves and straight work. The grit is water-fed on to a 24" soft steel-iron wheel. For inside curves I use 4" and 6" 100-grit crystal-ring diamond wheels. Most of our work involves small, fancy bevels, and these wheels work fine for them. I have even used a glass router head for rough-grinding small inside curves. When I can't get the curve this way, I use the edge of the 6" wheel, although this takes longer to stone out. I like working with diamond wheels because they are fast and clean.

For the second stage, the smoothing, I use a large man-made stone for outside curves and straight work. It is a hard stone and rarely needs to be trued. Of course, I have to take off the surface glaze now and then. A hard wheel works fine for small bevels of $\frac{1}{2}''$ wide or less. The wider bevels tend to hydroplane on a hard surface. A softer, natural stone seems to work better for wider bevels.

I do inside curves mostly on an aluminum-oxide cone wheel. I wouldn't be without it. Because most of my bevels are small, this stone suits me well. For big pieces, use the largest stone that you can to save time. The ideal would be to have two or more mandrels set up just for stone wheels. Then you don't have to keep changing stones, and they stay true longer.

The third stage, which is the messiest, is the first polish on the cork wheel. I use a large vertical wheel with a paddle-wheel system that we built ourselves. I like a paddle wheel because it keeps the cork evenly wet and charged. I use a 4F pumice mixture. I do both insides and outsides on the wheel, using the wheel edge for inside curves. The last stage—the final polish—calls for my solid 20-inch felt wheel and a high-grade cerium oxide mixture. On the sides of the felt wheel, I have two 10″ plates to help keep the soft wheel true. These wheels go out of true very easily if they are unguided. It is crucial that you keep your wheels trued.

For bead work, which is fun and simple, I usually use a $\frac{3}{4}$″ by 4″ aluminum oxide wheel. I dress the wheel so that it has a small elliptical face. You can vary the size of the bead by the pitch on the face of the wheel. This is easily done with a diamond dressing tool. Start at one end of the break line and work across it to the end. I like to honeycomb surfaces, although this can be tedious. Here I use a 10″ to 14″ wheel. It cuts fast, and I can get a smaller polishing wheel in each cut. Start honeycombing in one corner and work by rows, creating a honeycomb pattern containing rows of six-sided cuts.

I like to work with jewels, as you can see by my work shown in the color section. When I have calls for hand-cut jewels, I go to lapidary books, find the cut I am looking for, and adjust it to my needs. Lapidary books tell you which facets to cut first and how to work down a jewel. It takes time to cut a jewel, but when used correctly, they will enhance a window dramatically. I feel that they are worth all the effort and the time it takes to make them. Lapidary work and beveling have a lot of interchangeable parts. I study other crafts and try to see how many of them I can apply to beveling. But the main fun about beveling is just doing it. My advice is to always make your beveling as easy as possible to save yourself work, but never sacrifice quality.

I have a poster in my shop that expresses my feelings: "Happy are those who dream dreams and are ready to pay the price to make them come true."—L. J. Cardinal Suenens. At least for me this applies to glass—and to beveled glass in particular.

Ron Curtis: Magic Disks

I am a self-taught beveler and former college professor with degrees in psychology from UCLA and the University of Arizona.

I became interested in stained glass several years ago, and my transition from stained glass to beveled work was natural and gradual. I began by experimenting on a small lapidary machine, which I still use in conjunction with larger, horizontal equipment. Actually, I never used the lapidary machine for its own purpose. For my first two stations I use 24″ Somaca horizontal wheels.

I may be unique in that I never had a lesson in beveling, I never read a book on the subject, and never watched anyone work. I still haven't. I suppose there is an advantage to this because I haven't been caught up in any particular dogma. My feeling is that this can tie up your creative impulses.

My emphasis on beveled and engraved disks perhaps comes from my background in psychology. I am particularly fond of the *mandala*, the Sanskrit magic circle that signifies unity, perfection, completion. These paleolithic curves strike some sort of Jungian response in me, and I try to convey some of that feeling in my work. I like to combine beveled glass that has somewhat irregular fluid surfaces with corresponding pieces of stained glass. In the piece shown at center left on page 4 of the color section, I foiled $\frac{1}{4}''$ plate bevels with wavering borders to strips of a red antique to make a 12" circular panel.

Engraving is painstaking and tedious, but I think it pays off in the final aesthetic. At top right on color page 4 is a detail from a 12" disk made from $\frac{3}{8}''$ plate. I start to engrave from the front of the disk toward the center, making the pattern smaller as I go. I use an aluminum oxide stone and bring the work to a high polish.

My 9" disk with central jewel is shown at top left on color page 4. It is $\frac{3}{8}''$ plate with a 1" thick piece of slab glass, which I beveled into a cone. This fits into the central hole and is foiled. The engraving was done only toward the center here, and a clear area was left toward the rim. Note how the central jewel was shaped to stand out from the disk.

The color piece at bottom left, although it looks like a disk, was dish-shaped on my horizontal rougher. This piece is 9" in diameter and is made from $\frac{3}{8}''$ plate. I turned the circle and roughed from the rim toward the center, taking off more glass toward this area until I had a concave shape with a fairly thick rim and a much thinner center. This is fairly tedious work. When I had the shape, I took it to my smoothing stone and put the striations in with the edge of this wheel, again just turning the glass, barely touching it with the edge of the stone.

The last piece on my color page is a detail from a 4' by 2' arch using $\frac{3}{8}''$ plate. The cones are $\frac{1}{2}''$. This of course is more traditional beveling. Actually, I prefer bevels that don't follow the edge line. I usually strive for unusual optical effects in my centerpieces and panels.

Barbara Basham: Provocative Designs

For 20 years I worked as a registered nurse, and, in 1977, I took my first stained glass lessons. I had found the ultimate in hobbies. Although I loved the beautiful colors and textures of the stained glass, the beveled glass I began to see intrigued me even more. I started to incorporate the available machine bevels into my designs, adding a unique and fascinating dimension.

In 1979, I had an opportunity to work in a glass factory doing custom beveling—certainly different from nursing! There I was in my rubber boots and apron, covered with grit, grinding away and loving every minute.

At first I beveled only $\frac{1}{4}''$ clear. But I soon tried glue-chipped plate, Graylite plate, and then some samples of the chromatic colored, polished plate produced in Europe at the time. The colors were exquisite: amber, sapphire, topaz, dark green, quartz pink. Unfortunately, the glass was prohibitive to import. But I was fascinated with the idea of bevels and color.

Thick glass, especially $\frac{1}{2}''$, was a challenge. While it was difficult to cut and a little different to bevel (you need a steeper beveled plane and a lot more glass is ground away) I was dazzled by the intensity of the prisms, the vividness of the colors and just the sheer beauty of the bevel itself.

My first beveled window, the cornucopia (see color section) was produced at this time. I used $\frac{1}{2}''$ glue-chipped bevels for the border to give those wide and beautiful prisms. The design itself is simple—a rule I've tried to follow ever since. I want the bevels to do all the talking.

I decided to set up my own equipment at home, and my husband converted our patio into a studio. Lots of sun in Colorado and my studio faces South. Who could want anything more?

I contracted with David Meyer to design and produce my equipment. I needed 110 electrical units with a portable water supply at each wheel. As I worked with thicker and thicker glass, I discovered that it was more stable than thinner plate. I was concentrating on $\frac{3}{8}''$ and $\frac{1}{2}''$ and I could bevel very intricate designs with tight inside curves and long sharp points. I could bevel tiny pieces and still leave surface area. I discovered how to ''bank a curve'' in a way similar to a banked highway curve. For curves that go into long, sharp points, you have to bank the inside curve to give equal room for the outside bevel. This allows the angle to go right down the middle to the point and, with more of the glass preserved, it looks better.

I certainly had to come to terms with cutting, especially in the case of $\frac{1}{2}''$ glass. I began to learn the limits of my material—what it would and wouldn't do. For cuts other than gentle curves and straights, I had to devise a method. I covered my pattern pieces, front and back, with clear Contact paper, then taped the pattern to the glass right-side down with double-faced tape. I always beveled the side *opposite* the score. I tap, snap, pull, grozze and grind the glass until it fits the pattern. Using thick glass, the cutting and roughing stages take a long time. As I rough each piece, I lay it down on the pattern to see that the pieces fit together correctly. After I rough the bevels, I begin to cut the background glass. As I proceed with the beveling stages, I continue to fill in with background glass, so I can watch the window develop as I go along.

I like to use bevels as focal points, with a simple background composed of exquisite colored glass—usually antique, reamy, streaky, textured. In the design I worked out for the office of an eye doctor (see color section, page 2), I wanted a geometric, woven design that would still look like an eye. The panel had a practical use: to separate the nurse's office from the waiting room. The light in the waiting room is subdued and with extra light from the office, the bevels are shown to best advantage.

The window shown in the color section, page 3, was a real design challenge. I was commissioned to do eave windows with a Victorian theme above the main doorway of a private residence. I gave little forethought to the difficulty of the bevels in the main *fleur de lis*. To say the least, they were tricky.

To show how bevels can touch off interesting notions, another of my pieces is shown in the color section, page 3. This is a tribute to Jamie, my daughter, made when she was leaving for college. I wanted to do a Victorian girl in a black floppy hat with beveled plume and collar; I used my daughter's face in the cibachrome transparency and beveled the plume and collar. I am rather fond of the effect.

My next theme was botanical: three sunflowers gently nodding in the breeze. Each petal was beveled out of some prized yellow plate I was given. The glass was very hard and it took me forever to smooth it. The faces were beveled out of $\frac{1}{2}''$ bronze plate. The leaves were flashed glass and the background a medium-dark sheet antique. The faces were honeycombed to give the appearance of seed by The Wheel Engravers, a company specializing in glass engraving. They also gave the petals and leaves the effect of veins. A detail from this panel is shown on page 3 in the color section. The panel won Best of Show in the Glass at the Gardens exhibit in Denver.

I had made a stained glass lamp just to learn the techniques. Why not combine beveling with lampmaking? I began redesigning the plume I had made for the hat so it would fit half a lampshade. The bevels were large, and lamp pieces must be small to fit the curve. Believe me, I learned everything anyone has to know about soldering for this project, and then some. It was my third plume, so I had the bevels down pat—the fabrication was the nightmare. But in the end it all went together (see color section, page 2). I showed it at the Stained Glass Association of America summer convention in Boulder, where it won an award for Most Innovative Technique. I like that. It makes me anxious to try more innovative techniques.

Carl Powell: Extracts and Abstracts

My background is in art and I tend to think in terms of art, rather than in terms of any particular medium. Maybe that's why my approach is so startling to some traditionalists. I majored in painting at Georgia State, but became intrigued with the possibilities of stained glass. Everyone was turning out pretty traditional stuff and I thought, well, why not contemporary or avant garde in this medium? As an artist, I felt isolated in Georgia in 1975; I didn't really know what my "colleagues" might be doing.

I came across some old beveling equipment and began incorporating bevels into my stained glass panels. I was pretty sick of all that color in the traditional stained glass; I went for monochromatic hues in my work. I like photography, especially black and white. Looking at black and white negatives over long periods of time gives you a changed idea of color. I wanted clarity more than color, linearity as the focal point. (See color section, pages 10–12 for examples of Powell's work.)

I see my work as glass drawings. That linear quality, you know. I do a lot to emphasize it. I use different-sized leads, for instance, and a lot of black glass to complement the lead lines. I sandblast to give particular emphasis to areas, or just to provide background. I do contemporary designs and like my pieces to have one central focal point. I use clear double-strength glass to suspend other glass on. I epoxy glass to glass. How do I get my ideas? Well, I sketch a lot. I got into that habit as a painter, of course. I do a number of fast sketches, and then, when something hits me, I do a lot of designs. I work from a drawing standpoint and I have no hesitation in adding to a piece with paint or overleading. I'll use silicone to attach a portion of lead directly to the surface of the glass, I'll work with clear glass over clear glass so that it looks as though I've gotten an incredibly difficult cut. I'm interested in the effect and I'll go to any lengths to get it, stretch the medium to its utmost and, at that point, stretch it even further.

Titles? Well, the titles of my pieces don't really describe the pieces. They tend just to describe the titles. Linearity again.

What else? Well, I've been given a grant by the National Endowment for the Arts. I may be the first beveler to be so recognized . . .

Steve Williams: Skylight and Dome

A beveled skylight is an unusual item. Mr. and Mrs. Robert Redford came to me for something very colorful and dramatic for the ceiling of a large living room and it was my suggestion to use a lot of bevels. Ordinarily, you don't see bevels in a skylight. The Redfords were looking for stained glass and they thought that bevels were a good idea. The skylight is 15 feet by 5 feet, and is in a large living room with a high ceiling, more than two stories tall. There is a walkway below it. It has a southern exposure and, when you walk from one wing of the house to the other, the skylight is magnificent. After all, you're getting the sun from 20 points of light along a beveled surface. As you move, the sun follows you, appearing and reappearing in all those curved bevels. It's like a unified piece of cut crystal, filling the whole area with rainbows. The skylight has Thermopane glass about a foot and a half above it; dead air space serves for insulation.

Installation of the skylight presented some interesting technical difficulties. Chris McCall and I had driven to Ogden, Utah, to the Redford home, to install it. The local glass company I had contacted to help with scaffolding and installation was closed, and Redford decided he couldn't wait. He'd come from New York twice to see the thing installed. He rounded up a lot of guys, they rented a truck and scaffolding, and we installed the skylight that night, working pretty late. I'd fabricated it in two halves, with no center seam: to accomplish this, I'd beveled and cut the center pieces, then installed them in the frame so that I had an unbroken 15-foot span. I did *not* solder one juncture all the way down the center, so I could pull it apart, take out the pieces in the interstices, pack them up, take the whole thing to the job area, marry the two pieces and solder the center fifteen or so pieces back in. Sounds easy, doesn't it?

With the skylight in place, Redford didn't want to wait till morning to have his first look. He had lights installed on poles and on the chimney to get the effect right away. (See color page 5.)

The Redfords' skylight gave me the idea to do a beveled dome. The first job was to figure out geometrically what size sphere I wanted. I worked out the diameter and the depth, and from that extrapolated one section of a sphere of that dimension. That gives you the radius of curvature and that's the magic number you use to make everything. With that number you can divide the sphere into sections: I chose ten.

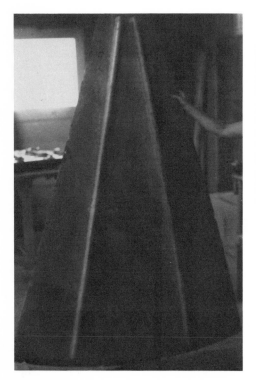

Fig. 12-2 Front of the mold shown in Fig. 12-1; the beveling design becomes a working pattern.

Fig. 12-1 Back of the mold for a single panel. The double curvature is seen from top to bottom, and from side to side; this furnished the basic shape of the dome.

Fig. 12-3 The pattern shown from the back of a panel.

Fig. 12-4 Reinforcing the back of each glass panel with vertical strips of galvanized steel helps to support the overall shape of the dome.

Fig. 12-5 Side view, showing the framework along the edge.

Fig. 12-6 The beveled dome being assembled in Steve Williams' studio. The bucket hangs where the central dome will be placed.

I wanted each section to have a compound curve—side to side, and up and down. Every other dome I've seen has been bent in only one direction. The side-to-side curve is not too obvious seen in the one section; you have to wait until you combine all the sections, then both curves become obvious and you have a sphere, not just flat bent panels. That is a subtle difference in a small project, but a notable one in larger scale.

The first thing I did was to make a plaster of paris form like a little bathtub, the size and shape of a single section. I shaped this out with a piece of metal on which I'd cut the radius. Now I had a measure for both curves. I filled the form with plaster and kept shaping it by scraping away the excess with my metal curve maker, until finally I was against the sides of the form all the way across, and was not removing any plaster. This meant the form had achieved the double curvature. I let the plaster harden. Please remember that I'm talking of two curves. If all I wanted was a single curve, I only had to take a straight piece of wood across the form and work off the excess and I'd have the single shape. But instead of the straight piece of wood, I made my other piece, the scraper, to the proper curve and worked with that over the plaster while it was still workable. When the plaster hardened it must have weighed about 250 pounds: I took it to an auto body place on my truck and sprayed both top and bottom to make a convex and a concave mold out of plastic. From these molds we made the framework. I'll tell you about that, but first the glass.

As the glass pieces are assembled, they must remain on the mold. These units are all curved. If the glass were not supported

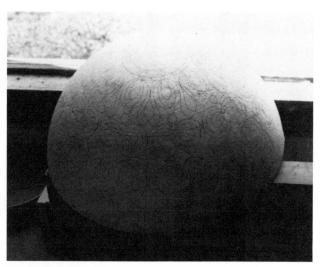

Fig. 12-7 A Styrofoam form of the dome-within-a-dome, showing the design for the bevels.

Fig. 12-8 The inner dome will eventually be placed within the larger one; the Styrofoam form is shown here.

by the mold, it would bend and crack of its own weight. The glass can't come off the mold until the brace bars are put on it. Since we must solder on both sides of the glass panel, when we turn the piece over the other mold is applied and we have a sandwich of glass between the two shaped molds. This way the glass can be manipulated safely.

As for the framework, I had all the metal rolled to that proper radius—that same magic number. This had to be done in a metal shop with the proper rolling equipment. Not many metal shops have the machinery for this, though every large city has at least one. The place I went to made boilers, so it had the equipment I needed. After the framework was rolled, the pieces were clamped together and every piece was modified until it all fit precisely. Then the pieces were welded and fabricated so that the whole can be taken apart in 10 sections.

Then I took the actual glass design and transferred it to the mold. This wasn't too difficult, since the compound curve in each section is so slight you could almost consider the sections flat. Of course there is a terrific amount of beveled glass involved. And everything must be letter perfect. This is a two-year project involving a lot of money.

The dome within the dome hangs inverted from the top. In the glass used for that, the bevels are actually curved to fit. They are not made from curved plate but are curved on the beveling machine. Just a slight bend is needed on the long pieces. On the top there will be a highly faceted lead crystal jewel. This 6″ wide, 4″ deep, leaded crystal jewel with 64 facets will go in the very center and has already been made by Mark Bogenrief, whose work also appears in the color section.

What will I do with the dome? Sell it, of course. I don't have a buyer as yet, but I'm not worried. Robert Redford? Well, he hasn't expressed interest. Yet.

Author's note: But the country of Kuwait has! (The completed dome is shown on the cover and in the color section, page 5.)

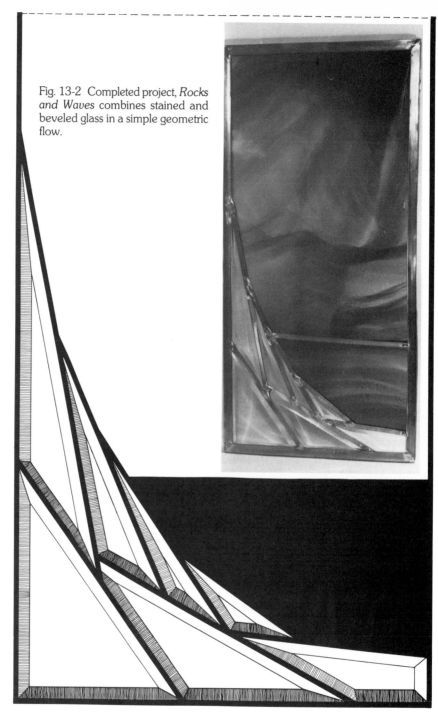

Fig. 13-2 Completed project, *Rocks and Waves* combines stained and beveled glass in a simple geometric flow.

Fig. 13-1 Pattern for *Rocks and Waves*.

PART III: Projects

◆━◇━◆━◇━◆━◇━◆━◇━◆━◇━◆━◇━◆━◇━◆━◇━◆━◇━◆━◇━◆

CHAPTER 13

Patterns and Processes

This chapter presents a number of ideas and projects at which you might wish to try your hand. In some instances, we provide a pattern which you may use as a guide to develop your own work. In other cases, we take you through projects from beginning to end. It is our hope that you will consider these part of the learning process, and certainly we trust that you will find all of them intriguing. We did.

Rocks and Waves

Rocks and Waves is a design for bevels and stained glass. The shape is strictly geometric, with more geometric shapes laid in. An interesting linear quality to a traditional design, made less traditional by the addition of the bevels. For the bottom portion of stained glass, "the sea," we used a deep-blue English streaky; the "sky" is a light-blue French streaky. Fig. 3-2, opposite, shows how the bevels stand out and how the line of bevels abruptly divides the two portions of the scene.

Straight-Wing Butterfly

We like butterflies and so, when we were invited to a party, we decided on a beveled one as a gift. This one now belongs to Lucy Freeman, a good friend who is not at all flighty.

To begin with, we made a pattern for the wings and body. Two steps in the production are seen in Fig. 13-3: the glass blanks of the upper wings and the roughed blanks of the lower wings. The notching of the wings was grozzed in first by hand, then emphasized with the diamond-wheel edge. These wings and the body (a glass chunk) were put through the entire beveling process and then put together just to get an idea of the placement of the pieces (Fig. 13-4). All pieces were then foiled (Fig. 13-5) and put together again to check how they were shaping up. You would be surprised to find how often foiling, especially poor foiling, will disturb the relationship of the pieces due to bumps and/or creases in the foil. It is better to find this out before soldering, so you can

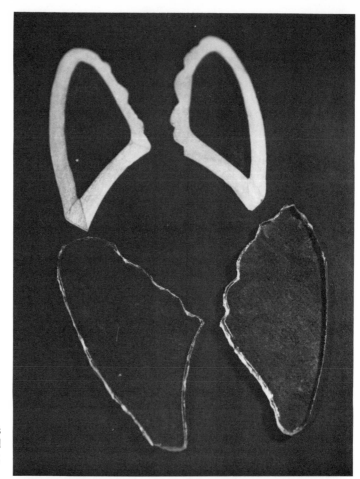

Fig. 13-3 Straight butterfly wings showing the grozzing and general shape. Above: after being roughed; below: the glass blanks.

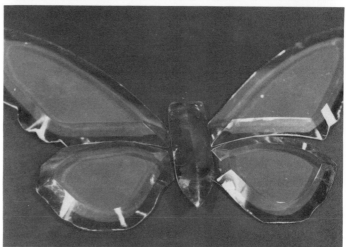

Fig. 13-4 The Straight-Wing Butterfly, with pieces assembled to show placement.

Fig. 13-5 The pieces foiled, but not soldered. We tried the body this way but did not like it.

Fig. 13-6 The Straight-Wing Butterfly, completed.

refoil. The foiling shown is pretty good: it conforms precisely to the glass edges and is even, top and bottom.

In Fig. 13-6, the finished piece is seen. Since bevels are heavy and foil is rather a delicate support, we used quite a lot of solder to hold the wings to the body. We also used a piece of brass below the body (you can see it through the body in the picture) which served the dual purpose of reinforcing the wings and providing a base for the little brass legs which you can't see. A hanging loop up front, soldered to the foil line below, adds to the shape of the head, and the antennae, made of thin brass wire, complete the project.

The idea was to make a panel which was both aesthetic and practical: ergo, a beveled mirror. Not a mirror beveled itself, but one surrounded by geometric bevels as a background. We began with the design seen in Fig. 13-7. From here we went on to make

The Beveled Mirror

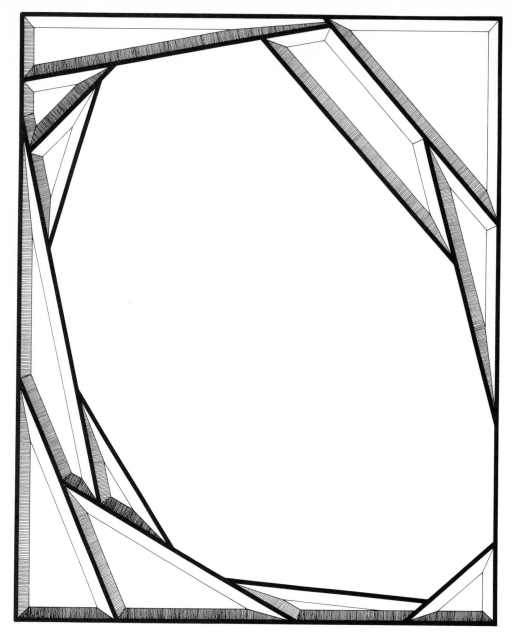

Fig. 13-7 Pattern for mirror with geometric bevels.

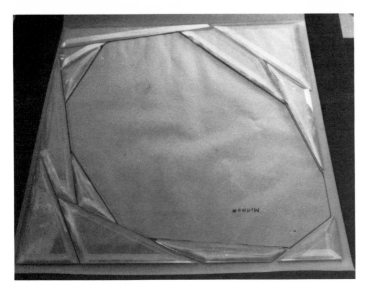

Fig. 13-8 The beveled pieces placed over the cartoon, the mirror portion yet uncut.

the bevels. These were placed over the cartoon for sizing (Fig. 13-8).

The next step was to cut the actual mirror without scratching the backing. This was placed in the center of our beveled pieces (Fig. 13-9). We used a brass-coated lead came furnished by Nervo International (see following section) to fasten all the pieces together and, since the solder joints were leadenly out of place against the brass, we plated them with the Kris Cal Plating Machine. The final result is seen in Fig. 13-10.

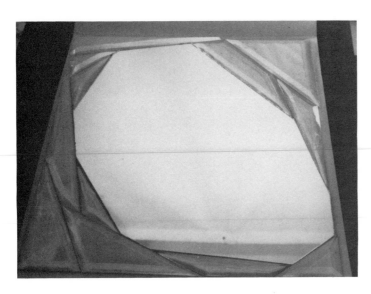

Fig. 13-9 The beveled mirror, pieces sized to pattern, mirror in place.

Fig. 13-10 The completed beveled mirror.

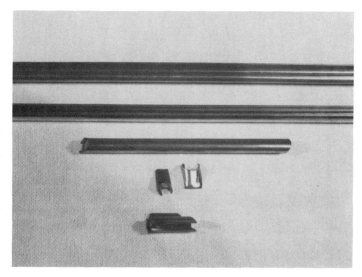

Fig. 13-11 Brass-covered lead channel is shown in straight lengths. It is available in H or U channel, as well as with angled channels. The last row but one shows at left, the lead came, at right, the brass plating that was over it. The brass is clipped very securely to the lead and we had to work to pry these two apart. (Courtesy Nervo International.)

Nervo International produces a brass-coated lead came that is a natural ally for beveled glass. In Fig. 13-11, the second row from bottom shows a small section of lead from which we have removed the brass. The came comes channeled and decorated to your taste; it is attractive and is not difficult to use on moderate curves. In fact, it behaves pretty much like lead came of the same diameter (Fig. 13-12). There are, however, two aspects of working with it that are different from lead came.

Working with Brass-Coated Lead Came

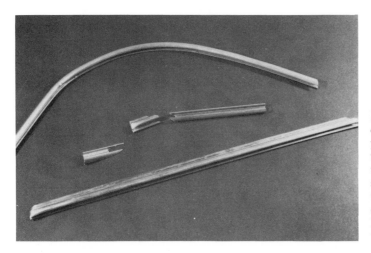

Fig. 13-12 Brass-coated came, an excellent material to use in beveled panels. It is rigid enough to maintain the form, yet pliable enough to make the necessary bends. The soldered joints must be brassed over to match the rest of the came on completion. This can be done with Rub and Buff, or by plating. (Courtesy Nervo International.)

Fig. 13-13 The easiest and most accurate way to cut brass came is to use the Window Works Electric Saw Came Cutter. It is a thoroughly delightful tool.

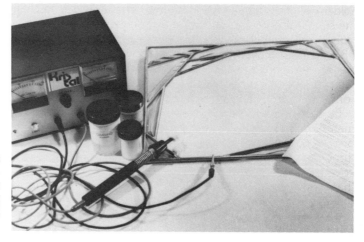

Fig. 13-14 Plating the joints of the brass-covered came with the Kris-tal-Electro-Plat-Tor. The effect is much more professional-looking than using Rub and Buff, and will last indefinitely.

While it can be mitred as one would mitre lead, the brass came cannot be cut properly without using a small saw. We have used a hacksaw with success, but this is cumbersome. The best way we have found to cut and mitre this came is with the Window Works Electric Saw Came Cutter shown in action in Fig. 13-13. This will cut any mitre you wish quickly and comfortably. It also does this with lead. An indispensable little tool which we cannot praise enough.

The second aspect of working with brass came involves the solder joints. Since the finish of the came is brass, the tin-lead

Fig. 13-15 Brass plating a joint with the anode of the Kris-tal-Electro-Plat-Tor. Cotton is wrapped around the graphite tip and, when this is dipped into the proper solution provided, and the current turned on, plating occurs. A fascinating process.

solder will stick out like a sore thumb. The answer is to change the color of the joints. This can be done adequately with Rub and Buff, but better still with the new Kris-tal-Electro-Plat-Tor in Fig. 13-14. This machine will plate almost any metal you would wish; we are using brass, but you are not limited to that. You will find the plating unit very simple to use and compact, as well as reasonably priced. Full instructions come with the machine.

Fig. 13-15 is a closeup of the way the anode from the Kris-tal machine is wrapped with cotton. This is then dipped into solutions provided, the machine clipped to the work, an electric current turned on. And behold! plating occurs as you swab the cotton-covered anode over the joints as shown. Not only is the effect that of a smooth, true plating, but it is fun to do.

Ideas are all around you and we use any number of sources for inspiration. We like animals and we like to doodle. Here are three examples of such doodling from Anita's sketchpad (Fig. 13-16). The beveled butterfly came from here. Of course, these are sketches, not cartoons, and must be modified for glass. But we find the modification comes later—if at all. Characterization is best expressed in the initial sketch. Calculating it for glass then requires some adaptation and you may occasionally find that it's impossible to execute your concept in glass. But doodling in this manner is restful and, at the same time, convinces you that you are actually working. Two other projects directly inspired by doodling follow.

Anita's Sketchbook

Fig. 13-16 Sketches provide ideas for possible beveled pieces.

Still Life: From Sketch to Panel

An apple and a pear are the subject matter in this still life. Beveled pieces are used in the foreground, and the background is composed of tints of stained glass. From this point, there are two ways to go: leave the piece as quiet and uncomplicated as it is, or make it more specific by adding paint lines to the glass that are seen in the sketch (Fig. 13-17). The problem is, the sketch is not beveled, nor can it be. One's perspective changes when one sees the glass in place. We favor just leaving it the way it is in Fig. 13-19, adding a stem to the apple with the leading. You may have different ideas.

Fig. 13-17 The original sketch for a beveled panel. We thought it would be interesting to see the transition from idea to completed product in a very simple production.

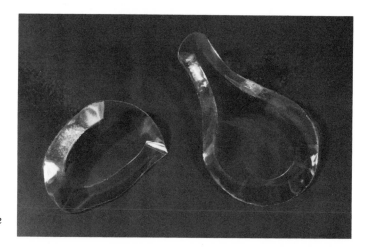

Fig. 13-18 The bevels: at right, the pear; at left, the apple.

196

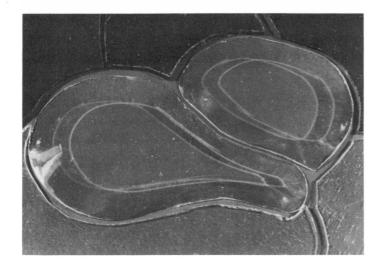

Fig. 13-19 Pieces of the still life in place, foiling and leading not yet done. The apple stem will be added with lead. Note how the bevels stand out from the background glass.

Bent-Wing Butterfly

The Straight-Wing Butterfly worked out so well that we decided to experiment with bending the wings. To our knowledge, no one had experimented with heating and bending beveled glass and we thought it would be nice to find out what effects we could get. The first thing to do was to get our configuration. This involved making the sketch, getting the proportions correct and making the shape. The basic shape was cut flat first, out of pattern paper. This was then outlined on the thinnest duct sheetmetal we could bend easily by hand. You can also use sheet copper or heavy tinfoil. Sometimes tin cans can be used. Just remove top and bottom with an opener, eat what is inside, and use the body for a butterfly form. Waste not, want not. We get our sheetmetal from scraps thrown away by a sheetmetal duct factory in our area. Sheetmetal is not as good as sheet copper for this work, but it will do and it is cheaper—even if you have to buy a piece.

Once the shape is outlined on the metal, use good tinsnips to cut it out. Ineffective tinsnips will make for a frustrating job, will ruin your outline, and may leave sharp slivers of metal for you to impale your fingers on. Once we had cut our metal in the flat, we bent it by hand to what seemed a reasonable and attractive curve. We then transferred the shape of the metal template to our mold material. You can use any mold material that is on the market. We use the powder recommended in *Stained Glass: Advanced Techniques* or the dental material recommended in our last book, *Crafting in Glass* (both published by Chilton). The powder is a combination of kiln wash, diatomaceous earth and calcium carbonate. We used the powder for this project since we always have it available.

Fig. 13-20 gives you an idea of some of the steps in this project. In the third row, you see the final bent and beveled glass wings.

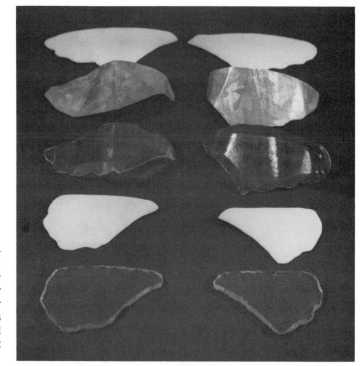

Fig. 13-20 At top, the oak tag patterns for the wings; below, the sheet-metal forms bent to shape. Below these, the actual bent glass upper wings. Fourth row, the patterns for the lower wings and, finally, the glass blanks for the lower wings—cut and grozzed, but not yet fired into a bent shape.

Fig. 13-21 The Bent-Wing Butterfly, with pieces placed to show how they will fit.

Fig. 13-22 The Bent-Wing Butterfly completed. The bevels and the bends reflect light nicely.

The glass was beveled prior to being placed in the kiln. One beveled piece was taken all the way through the operation to high polish. The other piece was only taken through the smoothing stone stage. Both pieces came out highly polished with no softening of the mitres. So, if you want to cut your beveling process short, you can put your smoothed pieces into the kiln and avoid the last two steps on your beveling machine. We're joking, of course. It would be impractical to do this (we believe). But the fire polishing of the bevels does work well. We took this particular plate glass ($\frac{3}{8}''$ new plate) to 1500°F to get the proper bend. The pieces were cooled rapidly, with the kiln top open (we used a top-loading kiln) to 900°F, and the kiln top was then closed. When the temperature registered below 300°F, we opened the top once more and allowed rapid cooling. The whole process, from putting the glass in to taking it out, is about $2\frac{1}{2}$ hours.

Fig. 13-21 shows the pieces placed for consideration of design and to achieve the most strength for foiling. Construction is a very necessary consideration since, as we have said, beveled glass is heavy and we are dealing with a fairly wide expanse here. The creature looks rather lifelike and the beveled wings throw the light about as though it were in flight.

The completed butterfly is shown in Fig. 13-22. In order to get the requisite strength, we used $\frac{1}{2}''$ foil and soldered it in two layers round the wings. We don't like to use this wide foil against a thin glass edge, but there was no help for it here. You might consider epoxying the wings and the body. A strong silicone might do the job and look better than the foil. We are still looking for the proper adhesive; so far, everything we have tried has not sufficed. Another way to avoid foiling might be to mount the butterfly upon an underlying circle of clear beveled plate, with the portions of the wings and body that touch it epoxied to it. You would want an epoxy that dried absolutely clear, of course. The point we want to make is, that just because we chose to foil the project doesn't mean there aren't other options open.

The Beveled Box

This beveled box is fun to make and provides experience in getting your bevels to match one another in a rectangle. The piece is laid out, as in any stained glass work, on a cartoon. Fig. 13-23 shows the pieces for the top placed in juxtaposition simply to get the effect. Here the bevels are merely roughed.

Fig. 13-24 shows the piece atop the numbered cartoon, with the finished, smoothed bevels. Alongside are some foiled opalescent glass flowers which are part of another project. The box was foiled except for the borders which, on the lid at least, were held with U-shaped brass came. Fig. 13-25 shows the lid resting on the box proper. The bottom of the box is a mirror. The sides of the box are themselves bevels, as shown in Fig. 13-26.

We chose to keep the lid and box separate; of course, you can hinge the lid to the box. The completed box, seen from the top, is shown in Fig. 13-27.

Fig. 13-23 Top of the beveled box, the bevels roughed and in place. The next step is smoothing.

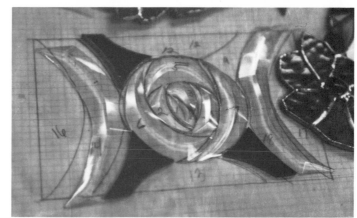

Fig. 13-24 The top of the beveled box being assembled on the cartoon. This top contains eight pieces of beveled plate.

Fig. 13-25 The bottom surface of the box is mirrored. The top can be left free or it can be hinged, whichever you prefer. The center jewel is a small beveled glass chunk.

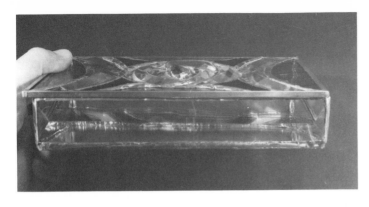

Fig. 13-26 Each side of the box is a pencil bevel, $1\frac{1}{2}''$ wide. Brass came was used for the borders of the lid.

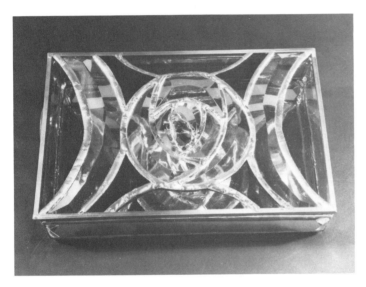

Fig. 13-27 The lid contains eight separate bevels of clear plate and measures 5″ by 8″ overall.

Foreground and Background

Fig. 13-28A demonstrates how a central beveled cluster enhances the look of what would otherwise be a rather bland window. Attention is immediately drawn to the central action of the design, seen as it would appear against a clear background. Actually, this foreground-background appearance is deceptive, for in Fig. 13-28B we see that the background is really glue-chipped, enhancing the beveled portion. Which effect do you prefer? Why not enjoy both? Experiment with projects of your own design to achieve a variety of foreground-background effects.

Fig. 13-28A Bevels against a background which appears to be clear glass.

Fig. 13-28B Actually, the glass is glue chipped, giving an altogether different impression of the background in closeup.

Fig. 13-29 A foreground made from bevels impressed with a "design" from factory-made plate glass. It is always fun to work with these materials, as the texture adds to the raised effect of the foreground bevels.

A great idea for pencil beveling is making letters and numbers. Doodling brought forth the plan of a designed alphabet and numbering system, as seen in Fig. 13-30. We don't mean for you to make all of these figures in pencil bevels—though it would undoubtedly make a spectacular display. You might, however, use some to spell a name or use a number. The advantage here is that they are all of the same design. If you don't like our design, go make your own and see if we care!

Beveled Alphabet Soup

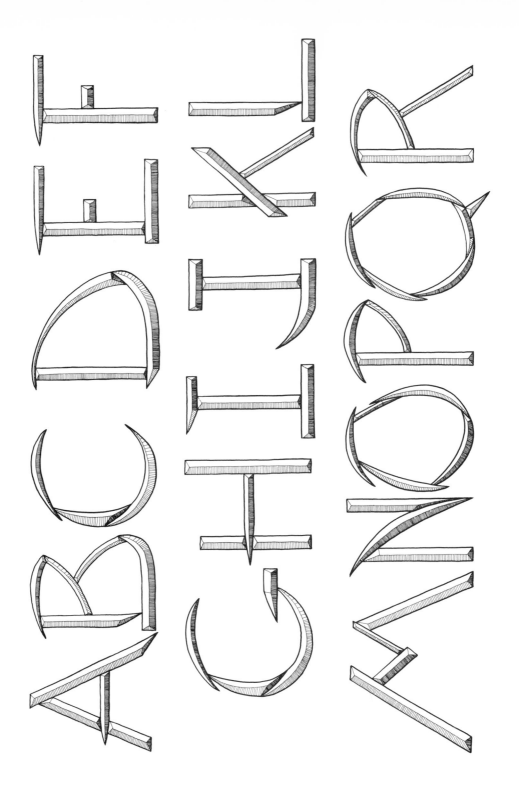

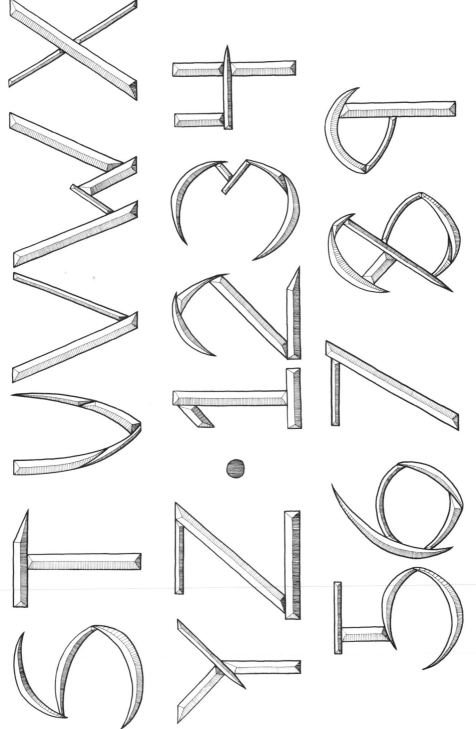

Fig. 13-30 Patterns for Alphabet Soup.

Man in the Moon

This is a unique project made by Linda Neely. It is one of our favorites. We assume that by this time everyone is familiar with how to make a paper-to-glass pattern, so we begin with the piece rough-grozzed and show you how to take it from there in Figs. 13-31 to 13-36. It would be a good idea to put a hole through the top of the glass with a diamond drill so that you needn't lead or foil the piece in order to hang it. Figs. 13-37 and 13-38 show the best way to cut the long strips of plate necessary for this project—another one of those practically indispensable tools.

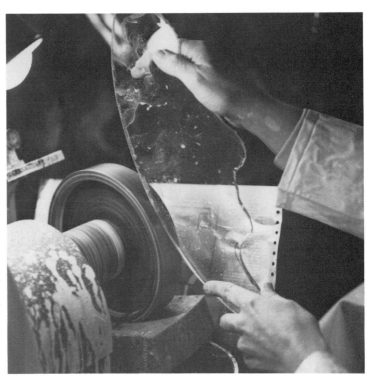

Fig. 13-31 Man in the Moon, with all major grozzing done. Minor grozzing, indicated by the ink lines below nose and chin, will be done to shape with a glass router.

Fig. 13-32 Shaping on the diamond wheel; this large piece of glass must be held and guided firmly.

Fig. 13-33 Using an Inland Craft's Wizard Grinder to get the final shaping of the Man in the Moon. Trying to grozze this type of detail by hand is possible but risky, as you can easily break the glass. Routers, such as the one pictured, have become an essential tool for most workers in glass. (See *Crafting in Glass* for descriptions of this and other routers and grinders.)

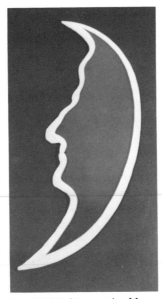

Fig. 13-34 Glass blank ground to the precise shape.

Fig. 13-35 Man in the Moon at the roughing stage.

Fig. 13-36 Man in the Moon, completed.

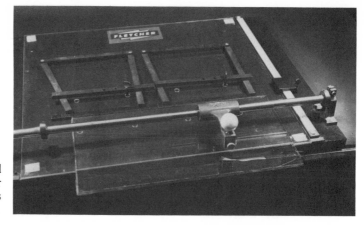

Fig. 13-37 The Fletcher horizontal cutting unit is an excellent tool for cutting long strips of plate. Glass is shown resting on the cutting board.

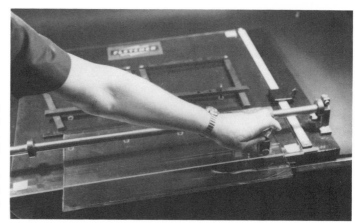

Fig. 13-38 Scoring glass with the Fletcher unit, demonstrating *only* the way the cutter is held. To actually cut the glass, the piece would be pushed up against the head stop, and the operator would stand below the board and support the glass with one hand while pulling the cutter toward him with the other.

Beveled Lamp

In Figures 13-39 and 13-40 we see how to produce an interesting three-dimensional object that is also practical, using bevels and a small amount of engraving. We engraved these panels freehand; you may use a guide if you wish. You can simply draw your design on the front side of the glass with a magic marker and follow the lines with the engraving wheel.

Fig. 13-39 One of four simple beveled panels with a graceful engraved figure in the center.

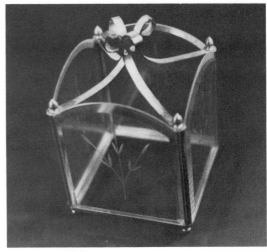

Fig. 13-40 The lamp uses four panels like the one in Fig. 13-39. The brass fixtures are obtainable in most good lamp stores.

Beveled Christmas Tree

This is a very simple project, but quite effective and a lot of fun. Fig. 13-41 shows what you can do for a decorative effect with beveling. The base was a piece of red antique glued to the tree ($\frac{3}{4}''$ clear plate).

Fig. 13-41 The Beveled Christmas Tree. The appearance of snow is achieved by leaving the bevel in the rough state. Notching was accomplished on the diamond wheel; if you don't have one, the edge of the cast-iron wheel will serve this purpose.

209

The Potted Plant

Another gluing project, though somewhat more ornate than the previous one. Figs. 13-42 to 13-44 show the processes. Framing such pieces adds a lot to their effectiveness. We made the project to fit a frame we already had. The pot consists of stained glass pieces. It is your choice whether to grout between them to give the appearance of lead lines. We rather prefer them spaced out.

Fig. 13-42 The beveled flowers placed on the cartoon to check design and fit.

Fig. 13-43 The beveled flower petals glued to the clear glass background.

Fig. 13-44 The final arrangement in a frame made by Morton Glass Works. Petal centers are crushed glass, glued—as are the petals—to the clear antique. *Caution:* Make sure you use a glue that dries clear; always test it on scrap glass first. It is also important to avoid trapping air bubbles in the glue, because they will show when the glue dries, alas. The flower stems were glued onto the reverse surface of the glass.

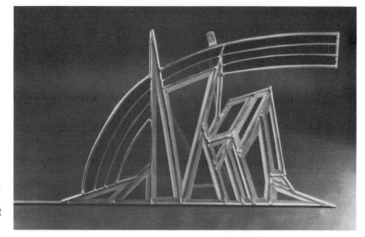

Fig. 13-45 Completed project, *Somewhere Under the Rainbow.* The bevels were designed to be left in the rough state.

Somewhere Under the Rainbow

We decided to try a free-flowing design, using strict geometric figures. The result looked, at least to us, like houses and spires, so we put a rainbow over them.

The design is shown in Fig. 13-46 and the finished product in Fig. 13-45. We decided not to polish any of the bevels here, sacrificing the subtlety of polished angles for a raw and powerful effect. This sort of modification is always your choice.

Fig. 13-46 Pattern for *Somewhere Under the Rainbow*.

Sources Of Supply

Beveling Machines

Denver Glass Machinery, Inc.
1804 S. Pearl St.
Denver, CO 80210

Maja Mining and Manufacturing Co.
9553 De Soto Ave.
Chatsworth, CA 91311

Bevelcrafter
Kindig Enterprises
1904 Serge Ave.
San Jose, CA 95130

AIT Industries
2020 Hammond Drive
Schaumburg, IL 60195

Sommer & Maca Industries
5501 W. Ogden Ave.
Chicago, IL 60651

Brass-Coated Lead Came

Nervo International
650 University Ave.
Berkeley, CA 94710

Glass Routers

Glastar Corp.
19515 Business Ctr. Dr.
Northridge, CA 91324

Kindig Enterprises
1904 Serge Ave.
San Jose, CA 95130

Inland Craft Products Co.
1470 Temple City Dr.
Troy, MI 48084

Preformed Bevels

Cherry Creek Enterprises
937 Santa Fe Drive
Denver, CO 80204

Bevels, Ltd.
4676 Admiralty Way
Suite 719
Marina Del Rey, CA 90291

Nervo International
650 University Ave.
Berkeley, CA 94710

The Glass Bevel
3823 E. Anaheim St.
Long Beach, CA 90804

Beveling Instructors and Repair Services

Denver Glass Machinery, Inc.
1804 S. Pearl St.
Denver, CO 80210

214

Anita Isenberg
PO Box 244
Norwood, NJ 07648

Linda Neely
581 S. University Blvd.
Denver, CO 80209

Temick Glass Studio Ltd.
809 E. Gloria Switch Rd.
Lafayette, LA 70507

Glass Lathes

Sommer and Maca Industries
5501 W. Ogden Ave.
Chicago, IL 60650

Colored Bevels

The Glass Bevel
3823 E. Anaheim St.
Long Beach, CA 90804

Steven R. Johnson
3441 N. Prospect
Colorado Springs, CO 80907

Glasscutting Equipment

The Fletcher-Terry Co.
Spring Lane
Farmington, CT 06032

Glass Accessories International
10112 Beverly Dr.
Huntington Beach, CA 92645

Morton Glass Works
Box 465
170 E. Washington
Morton, IL 61550

Glass Pliers

Diamond Tool and Horseshoe Co.
4702 Grand Ave.
Duluth, MN 55807

Glass Suppliers

S. A. Bendheim Co.
122 Hudson St.
New York, NY 10013

Bullseye Glass Co.
3722 S.E. 21st Ave.
Portland, OR 97202

Buffalo Plate & Window Glass Corp.
1245 E. Ferry St.
Buffalo, NY 14211

Kokomo Opalescent Glass
PO Box 2265
1310 S. Market St.
Kokomo, IN 46901

Frames

Pop-Lock
6814 Humboldt Ave. No.
Brooklyn Center, MN 55430

Plating Equipment

Kris-tal
PO Box 662
Gig Harbor, WA 98335

Colored Glass Dalles

Cecil Wilson
H.C.H. Chemicals
Long Beach, CA 90804

Blenco Glass Co. Inc.
Milton, WV 25541

Beveling Wheels

The Carborundum Co.
Niagara Falls, NY 14302

Brass-Came Cutters

The Window Works
PO Box 1643
Weaverville, CA 96093

Silicon Carbide & Pumice

Salem Distributors
2036 Stratford West Blvd.
Winston Salem, NC 27103

Appendix

There are machines other than those produced by Denver Glass which may work well for you. Unfortunately, the scope of this book does not permit our evaluating these machines in depth, though we would very much have liked to. We will, at least, take the time to describe three of them.

The Somaca Glass Lathe and Glass Polisher

These are two separate units. The glass lathe is designed for mounting on a bench or table for the convenience of the operator. It can be used with a wide variety of wheels for engraving glass-ware, mitring, grinding of inside curves, and edging holes. It uses wheels and a cone stone.

A word about cones. We haven't stressed them in this book, but they can be very useful. We find that diamond cones, in

The Somaca Beveling Lathe. Courtesy of Sommer and Maca Industries.

particular, are great for inside curves. You can get a cone for any side arbor. (Order them from the Carborundum Co. in Niagara Falls.) The cone is made to screw into the particular arbor you have. It does take rather a while to get delivery; at least, that has been the experience of many workers.

The Somaca Glass Polisher is, in reality, a separate felt-wheel unit used with cerium oxide. If you are using it as part of the beveling protocol, you must get the other stations as well.

Maja Diamond Glass Beveling Machine

This is a horizontal wheel/cone beveler using industrial-grade diamonds; wheels range in size from 8″ to 18″ in diameter. Diamonds cover the entire surface of the working areas. Although

Diamond glass-beveling machine. Made by Maja Mining and Manufacturing Co.

we ourselves have not worked the unit, the demonstration we saw at Glass Expo was commendable. The horizontal wheels have a grooved surface which, according to the manufacturer, speeds up the beveling procedure. The machine is lightweight and appears to be sturdy. This is a hand-held unit. The motors are variable in speed, allowing a great deal of control during the beveling procedure. You can do straight bevels, as well as inside and outside curves. Although the manufacturer claims unlimited design capabilities, this is true of almost any type of beveling unit. The manufacturer told us he couldn't make the units fast enough. It is an indication of the tremendous interest that has recently been aroused in beveling.

Kindig Enterprises' Bevelcrafter

This machine, according to the manufacturer, utilizes the highest level of industrial diamond technology to produce a grinding head capable of removing glass efficiently and exactly to the prescribed angle and bevel width desired. A rough diamond grinding head removes 98% of the required glass. This is followed by a finer diamond-coated beveling head, preparing the glass for stage III diamond or abrasive finishing. Felt polishing with optical polishing

The four-station Bevelcrafter: the felt wheel is the only vertical component. When smoothing a beveled edge with the Bevelcrafter, the glass lies flat on the steel plate of the machine. This allows for few facets to form as the glass is literally locked into place. To the left is seen the roughing wheel. Courtesy of Kindig Enterprises.

compound renders the bevel crystal clear. The glass always lies flat and is simply moved across the fixed angle diamond grinding head to achieve accurate, perfect bevels of any shape. This is, therefore, not a hand-held unit, the only such type to appear in this book.

The polishing unit of the Bevel-crafter is similar to the vertical stations of other units. Here the glass is hand-held against the wheel. Courtesy of Kindig Enterprises.

Index